VOLUME 6

MESSERSCHMITT
Me 262 STURMVOGEL

By Dennis Jenkins

PUBLISHERS AND WHOLESALERS

Published by
Specialty Press Publishers and Wholesalers
11481 Kost Dam Road
North Branch, MN 55056
United States of America
(612) 583-3239

Distributed in the UK and Europe by
Airlife Publishing Ltd.
101 Longden Road
Shrewsbury
SY3 9EB
England

ISBN 0-933424-69-8

Material contained in this book is intended for historical and
entertainment value only, and is not to be construed as usable
for aircraft or component restoration, maintenance or use.

Designed by Greg Compton

Printed in the United States of America

TABLE OF CONTENTS

THE MESSERSCHMITT Me 262 STURMVOGEL

PREFACE

Numerous excellent, and some not so excellent, books have been written about the Me 262 and its effect on the outcome of World War Two. It is interesting to compare the various works, and to note that very few of them agree on any given detail. First flight dates, pilots names, and locations are often different in each book, not necessarily by days, but occasionally by months! I have attempted to sort out the confusion by checking data against what few official records still exist, but it is totally possible some data is incorrect.

Contrary to most popular opinion, even fifty years later, I believe the consensus of researchers is that the airplane, and the decisions concerning it, did not have a material impact upon the outcome of the war. Less than 200 Me 262s were in operational service at any one time, despite the almost heroic efforts of Messerschmitt to manufacture over 1,400 of them within 18 months.

The problems lay not with the aircraft, or even with the political decisions concerning its role and manufacture. The problem was simply one of technology. Junkers could not produce enough engines, especially enough reliable engines, to power all the airframes that Messerschmitt was capable of building. The Allies certainly influenced this problem. Heat-resistant metals were difficult to obtain in Germany towards the end of the war. Constant bombing raids disrupted production and distribution of critical parts. Completed airframes were strafed and bombed before the could be delivered.

Simply put, even if Hitler had allowed the Me 262 to enter production without change, Junkers could not have produced sufficient engines to power them.

And although the Me 262 is usually portrayed as being the forbearer of many advanced designs, it was actually very much a compromise aircraft. It designers were not particularly happy with many aspects of it. The 'advanced' swept-wing was an inelegant solution to a late engine change. The underslung nacelles were a solution of oversized and overweight powerplants. The aircraft had zero serious wind-tunnel time, and a disappointingly low critical Mach number. Its designers were not supermen changing the world, but good, competent engineers responding to events largely out of their control.

This work will attempt to cover the early development and production variants of the Me 262. It will not attempt to cover the operational aspects any further than absolutely necessary since there are several excellent books already extant on that subject (most notably *The Me 262 Combat Diary* by John Foreman and S. E. Harvey). Likewise the immense efforts that were put into building a manufacturing base for the aircraft are only briefly explored here, but are thoroughly covered in Hugh Morgan's *Me 262: Stormbird Rising*. And finally, the Allied use of captured Me 262s after the war (*Watson's Wizards*, etc.) deserve a book of its own, such as *War Prizes* by Phil Butler. A selected bibliography appears at the end of this text.

DESIGNATIONS AND SERIALIZATION

German designations differ somewhat from the standard USAF form. In the case of the Me 262, the 'Me' obviously represents Messerschmitt AG, while the '262' is a type number assigned by the RLM. The first production variant adds an 'A' (Me 262A), while the first major sub-variant adds another number (Me 262A-1), and minor sub-variants add an additional lower case character (Me 262A-1a). Field modifications are usually identified by 'U' numbers appended to the factory designation (Me 262A-1a/U1). As in other Air Forces, this scheme was not always followed as diligently as historians would like.

The standard method of identifying individual aircraft involves two separate schemes. The first is the *Werknummern* (*Werk-Nr.*) assigned by the manufacturer with the concurrence of the RLM. This serial number number is used to in maintenance manuals, etc., to differentiate production changes, etc. In an effort to confuse Allied intelligence services, these numbers were not always consecutive, and gaps were frequently left to make the production run look larger than it was. In addition, aircraft receive *Stammkennzeichen* alphanumeric coding in the form 'xx+yy' that carries sig-

nificance about the unit the aircraft is assigned to, etc.

It is usual procedure for German prototypes to carry *Versuchs* numbers (V1, etc.) in their designations (Me 262V1, etc.). For the Me 262, this initially covered the first ten machines. However, following fairly high losses during the test program, various production aircraft were allocated back to Messerschmitt for use in continued testing. At first these machines were reassigned *Versuchs* numbers of machines that had been lost (*Werk-Nr.* 130015 was redesignated V1, 170056 was V2, and 170303 was V7, etc.) Later, to avoid further confusion, the production machines simply took the last three digits of their *Werknummern* as their V-numbers (170056 became V056, etc.). Among the test aircraft in this series were V074, V083, V167, V186, and V555.

The *Luftwaffe* assigned all jet and rocket engines into the family numbered 109, with each manufacturer's specific product given a sequential number after this—BMW was assigned 109-003 and Jumo 109-004. Generally it is accepted to put the manufacturer's name ahead of the sequential number and to ignore the 109. Major variants and sub-variants are designated similar to aircraft types as described above.

ACKNOWLEDGEMENTS

The author would like to thank the following for the assistance they rendered in preparing this publication: Jay and Susan Miller; Herbert and George Tischler of the Texas Airplane Factory; Henrik Clausen; Wesley B. Henry and Dave Menard from the Air Force Museum; David. E. Brown; and Dick Holbert and the staff of the Arkansas Aerospace Education Center.

Dennis Jenkins
1996

THE Me 262

The Eighth Air Force fighter pilot who caught up with this twin-jet enemy aircraft over Germany had all the instincts of a recognition expert, for as he fired a series of bursts, he photographed it from half-a-dozen angles, thus providing a group of pictures which give the best idea to date of the appearance of this new plane.

The first publicized photographs of the Me 262 were these gun camera shots from an Eighth Air Force P-51 Mustang. About the only time a Mustang was assured of being able to 'kill' an Me 262 was when the Swallow was landing or taking-off, since the turbojet engines did not respond well to rapid throttle movements. During normal flight, the Me 262 could simply outrun Allied fighters. (Air Force Museum Collection)

HATCHING THE SWALLOW

As early as 1863, Frenchman Jean Delouvier proposed a jet propulsion system for aircraft, and by 1909 several French patents had been issued to various individuals. In 1930, Flying Officer Frank Whittle was awarded British patent number 347206 for an engine consisting of an axial compressor, a subsequent radial stage, combustion chamber, axial turbine, and a circular arrangement of thrust nozzles. Regardless of the earlier patents, of which Whittle was probably unaware, the British are generally credited with the invention of the modern turbojet engine.

On 10 November 1935 Hans Joachim Pabst von Ohain was awarded German patent 317/38 for a jet engine he had developed while a student at Göttingen University. In April 1936, aircraft manufacturer Ernst Heinkel hired von Ohain and provided him with a laboratory to continue his work. In September 1937, Dr. von Ohain successfully ran the first prototype of

An Me 262A-1a (Werk-Nr. 111711) shows the features that made it famous. A thin swept-wing optimized for high-speed flight, and turbojet engines enclosed in underwing nacelles. Both innovations were the result of late changes in the choice of engines, and not conscious efforts to control the effects of compressibility. (Air Force Museum Collection)

the Heinkel S2 hydrogen-powered turbine engine.

The Bavarian Motor Werks (BMW) had also begun designing a jet engine in the late 1930s when Dr. Kurt Löhner and Dr. Müller Berner of BMW GmbH in Munich had commenced studies on a centrifugal-type engine designated F9225-TL. However, following the takeover of the Brandenburgischen Motorenwerke GmbH (Bramo) by BMW in September 1939, the F9225-TL was discarded in favor of the P.3302 axial-flow design which had originally been conceived by Bramo in Berlin-Spandau. The engine was expected to produce 1,320 LBF static thrust (or about 1,580 LBF at 560 MPH), and to be available for flight testing by the end of 1939. Directing the effort was Dr. Hermann Ostrich, who had been investigating jet propulsion since 1928.

At the Magdeburg branch of the Junkers Motorenwerke AG, Professor Herbert Wagner outlined his ideas for a turbojet engine. Due to internal conflicts within various Junkers companies, and the complex design of Wagner's axial-flow powerplant, this program got off to a slow start. When the internal politics finally got sorted out, it was Junkers Motorenbau (normally abbreviated Jumo) that was authorized to commence design work on the 1,500 LBF s.t. T1 turbojet in 1939 under the direction of Dr. Anselm Franz. Unlike the BMW engine, which was techni-cally sophisticated and elegant from an engineering perspective, the Jumo engine was intended to be simple, both in design and manufacture. First units were expected to be available for flight tests in mid-1940.

HATCHING THE *SWALLOW*

In late autumn of 1938, the *Technisches Amt* (Technical Department) of the *Reichsluftfährtministerium* (RLM—German Ministry of Aviation) approached Willy Messerschmitt and Ernst Heinkel to study the feasibility of building a jet-propelled aircraft utilizing the new *TL-Strahltriebwerke* engines. It should be noted that the RLM did not specify a role that the aircraft should be designed to perform, leaving this choice to the manufacturers. In fact, it appears that the RLM would have been content with a strictly experimental aircraft at this point.

The Messerschmitt team elected to use the BMW engine to begin designing their new aircraft, primarily because it was expected to be available first. The aim of the Messerschmitt team led by Dr. Woldemar Voigt was simple—produce the fastest possible fighter aircraft. Messerschmitt had first received information regarding the *TL-Strahltriebwerke* engines during 1937, and as early as October 1937

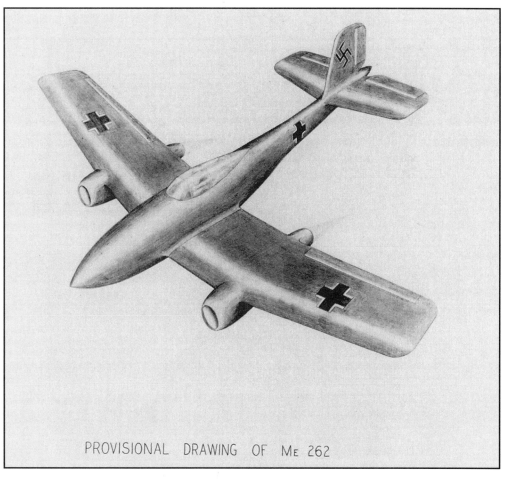

PROVISIONAL DRAWING OF Me 262

A 1943 drawing shows what the Americans believed the Me 262 would look like. This drawing was based on minimal intelligence, but proved to be remarkably accurate. (Air Force Museum Collection)

had conducted trade studies to determine the relative advantages of a twin engine jet fighter over a single engine aircraft. Due to the expected limited power of the new turbojets, the earliest designs featured two engines to obtain sufficient thrust. However, Messerschmitt and Voigt did not feel comfortable with this for a 'true' fighter, and discarded the design in favor of a concept powered by a single BMW P.3302 (later redesignated 109-003, or BMW 003).

In this design, the air intake was mounted in the extreme nose with the engine exhaust in the tail, similar to many post-war designs (F-84, MiG-15, etc.). The major disadvantage was the amount of fuselage necessary to cover the intake and exhaust ducting while still main-taining a reasonable center of gravity. It was felt that the ensuing weight was likely to be prohibitive, and the large wetted area of the intake tract would lead to a reduction in total pressure, failing to take complete advantage of the BMW engine's limited power.

In an effort to solve these problems, Messerschmitt created a twin-boomed aircraft that looked remarkably similar to the later British de Havilland Vampire. With the engine located in the short center nacelle, many of the problems with the original design were solved. However, the design was not considered optimal in an aerodynamic sense, and the total external wetted area was substantial, leading to significant drag and a limited top speed.

The replacement for the twin-boom design was a pod and single-boom arrangement, similar to the post-war Bell X-5 and Yak-17. The pilot and armament were located on top of the engine, and the fuselage was contoured around these installations before terminating in a long, thin boom designed to hold the rear-mounted vertical and horizontal stabilizers. Unusual, at least for the period, was the tricycle undercarriage (instead of the more 'conventional' tail-dragger). It was the landing gear that would ultimately lead to the dismissal of the design. The problem was not that it was a tricycle design, but that there was no logical location to retract it into. All the designs considered led to an overly complicated installation that interfered seriously with either the engine installation or the

The Swallow was an extremely clean aircraft, as shown by this Me 262A-1a (Werk-Nr. 111711) being test flown over Wright Field on 12 September 1945. By this point the aircraft had been stripped of its paint, although German markings have been reapplied for unknown reasons. (Air Force Museum Collection)

fuselage–wing interface. A conventional tail wheel configuration could not be adapted since it would be directly in the engine exhaust.

Having reasonably dismissed the possible designs for a single engine fighter, Messerschmitt and Voigt turned again to the original twin engine concepts. They were still not happy with the idea since they believed that a two-engine aircraft would increase the weight, power, and size requirements to a point that the aircraft would be ineffective as a fighter. But they still realized that the limited power of the first jet engines might force them into utilizing two to obtain the necessary power-to-weight ratio. Also, the use of two engines appeared to simplify the design, especially of the landing gear.

Keeping the design simple was a primary goal of the exercise. The rationale was twofold. First, the aircraft was going to pioneer a radical engine concept, and Messerschmitt wanted to minimize other variables. This was much the same rationale that led to the conservative American design for the Bell P-59A. Secondly, it was obvious that Germany would soon be at war, and it was necessary to produce a design that was easy to manufacture and simple to maintain.

The first Messerschmitt two-engined design featured the engines buried in the wing roots.

ISSUED WITH A-I-2 (G) REPORT NO. 2292   DEC. 44   DRAWING NO. X 147   RESTRICTED

A late-1944 drawing was much more accurate, primarily because the Allies had actually captured several Me 262s on gun camera film. (Air Force Museum Collection)

But as more details became known about the size and weight of the BMW engines, this began to look impractical. Soon, two variations of a different twin-engine aircraft emerged. Both designs were all metal monoplanes with an engine submerged in the straight wing at approximately quarter-span. What differentiated the designs was the placement of the wing. The mid-wing design was promising from an aerodynamic perspective, but its placement forced a complex landing gear retraction mechanism. Also, Messerschmitt predicted that the manufacturing costs of the design would be prohibitive, and that repairs under operational conditions would be difficult at best. The second design was for a low-wing monoplane that greatly simplified the undercarriage design.

On 7 June 1939 Messerschmitt and Heinkel submitted their concepts to the RLM. The He 280 featured many revolutionary concepts, such as a compressed-air ejection seat (the first such design) and a pressurized cockpit. Its fully retractable tricycle landing gear enabled it to taxi with its axis horizontal, the thrust from its two He S8A turbojets directed straight backwards, parallel to the ground. In all, an elegant design, although a heavy one predicted to be of less-than-spectacular performance.

The Messerschmitt *Projekt 1065* proposal outlined an all-metal low-wing cantilever monoplane powered by two BMW 003 engines. The aircraft was 30.5 feet long with a wing span of 30.83 feet and a height of 9.19 feet. The maximum flying weight was 9,527 pounds, with a landing weight of 7,047 pounds. A speed of 560 MPH was expected at an altitude of 9,843 feet (3,000 M). The conventional tail wheel undercarriage was arranged so that the main wheels retracted partly through the wing, with the tail wheel retracting into the rear fuselage. In order to provide an aerodynamic fairing for the retracted wheels within the thin wing, the fuselage was given a triangular cross-section, the base of the triangle being wide enough to incorporate the wheel wells. This also led to a good field of vision from the cockpit as the apex of the triangle was near the pilot's eye level, and minimized the induced drag between the fuselage and the wing. The wing passed through the the wide fuselage base and was an all-metal structure with a single built-up I-section main spar and flush-riveted stressed skin. The engines were submerged in the wings at approximately quarter-span and the outer wing panels incorporated a small degree of sweepback on the leading edge. Nearly full-span automatic leading-edge slots and Frise-type ailerons were fitted.

Just before submitting their proposal to the RLM, the Messerschmitt team made two critical modifications to P.1065—they doubled the aircraft's endurance from 30 minutes to one hour; and they increased the armament to four 30mm cannon with provisions for two additional weapons. Voigt's team believed these modifications would create a better fighter, thereby making the design more attractive to the RLM. Space was also reserved to fit an ejection seat, although little research had been conducted on exactly how to accommodate one.

After evaluating the two designs, the RLM declared Messerschmitt the winner, and the company received a contract to continue development. But the RLM had seen promise in both proposals, and the Heinkel design also

The remains of several Me 262s inside the assembly hall at Obertraubling. At least nine nose section are lined up against the far wall. The only identifiable aircraft is Werk-Nr. 500488, which is laying on the ground in front of the observer. (Air Force Museum Collection)

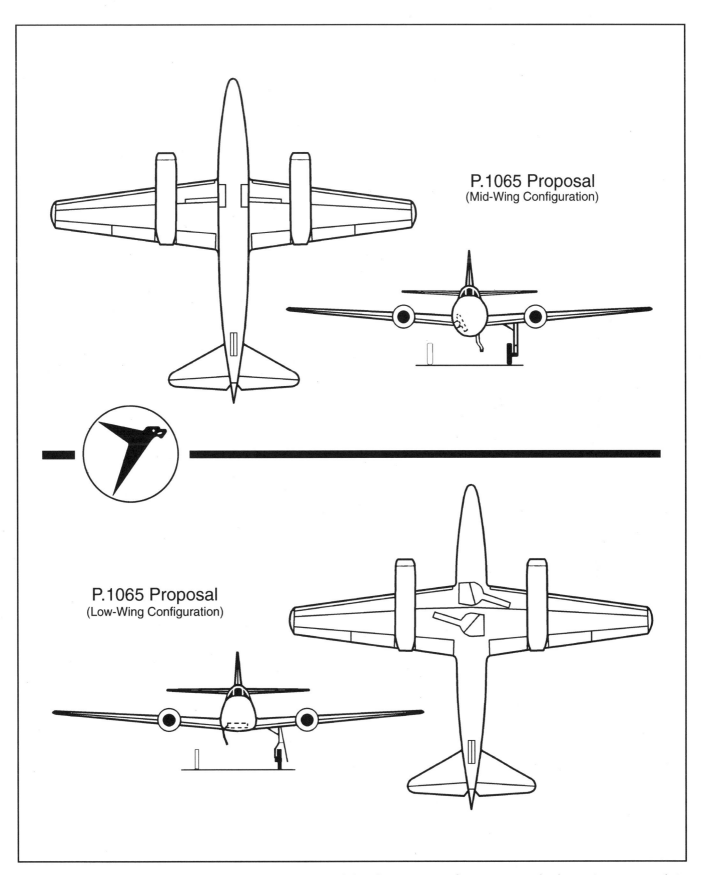

P.1065 Proposal
(Mid-Wing Configuration)

P.1065 Proposal
(Low-Wing Configuration)

The two P.1065 proposals. Noteworthy is the staggered landing gear configuration on the low-wing proposal. At this point both concepts featured basically straight wings with the engines submerged at quarter span. There is very little resemblance to the eventual Me 262. (Dennis R. Jenkins)

received continued support. On 2 April 1941, the He 280 would become the first of the two designs to fly. In fact, on the day of the Me 262's first flight, underpowered by a piston engine, the He 280 would set a world's speed record of 485 MPH.

As an aside, the first flight of a jet aircraft in Germany had taken place two years earlier. On 27 August 1939, just three days before the outbreak of World War II, the He 178 test aircraft had first flown powered by a single 1,100 LBF He S3B turbojet engine. The flight was conducted by *Flugkapitän* Erich Warsitz at the Rostock-Marienehe airfield. This small aircraft was not capable of performing any militari-ly useful roles, but did serve as an excellent test-bed for Heinkel.

Following the RLM acceptance of the P.1065 proposal, the Messerschmitt designers set out to validate their earlier findings, and on 9 November 1939 submitted a slightly improved design for approval. Work then commenced on building various mock-ups of the design, and after an examination of the mock-ups by the RLM on 1 March 1940, Messerschmitt received a contract to build four examples of the new aircraft. Three of the airframes would be used for flight testing, while the fourth would be a static test article, explaining why most sources report the contract was for three aircraft. The new design would be known as the Me 262.

On 15 May 1940 another design revision was submitted to the RLM with two major changes that would mark the beginning of the Me 262 as it would finally emerge. Initial bench tests of the BMW engine had resulted in only 570 LBF thrust, forcing BMW into a major redesign of the powerplant. In April 1940 BMW finally admitted that the jet engine would be substantially larger and heavier than had been predicted. This presented the Messerschmitt team with a serious center-of-gravity problem. Since the design of the aircraft was considered too far along to affect major changes, the Messerschmitt engineers devel-

One of the 50MM cannon equipped Me 262s photographed at Melun, France on 3 May 1945. The modified nose landing gear rotated the nose wheel so that it lay flat to provide clearance for the weapon. (Air Force Museum Collection)

oped what they considered a rather inelegant fix to the problem. They added a truly swept outer wing panel, moving both the center-of-gravity and center-of-pressure rearward. This was considered easier than redesigning the fuselage to move the entire wing aft. So although the Me 262 is widely heralded as a landmark design because of its swept wing, it actually reflected no attempt to reduce the effects of compressibility, but was a rather a simple fix to a weight problem. In fact, the Me 262 would prove to be exceptionally unstable in the transonic regime.

The second major change was the placement of the engines themselves. The original P.1065 had the engines submerged in the wings, much like the later British Gloster Meteor, greatly complicating the design of the wing structure. Now, with the revised estimate from BMW of engine size and weight, the turbojet's diameter was simply too large to effectively place within the wing. Again, the Messerschmitt designers opted for the easiest solution—moving the engines under the wings instead of in them. This configuration left the upper wing surface undisturbed by the engine nacelle, while the lower wing surface was flush with the fuselage bottom. This significantly improved the aerodynamics and led to a slight increase in total lifting surface. Another appealing feature was that the upward displace-

ment of the fuselage with respect to the engine nacelles increased the distance between these bodies, and thus reduced the possibility of flow interference between them. The arrangement would prove not only lighter and less costly than the in-wing design, but also afforded a decrease in overall drag.

Thus was born the 'revolutionary' Me 262 that so intrigued Allied forces during the closing days of the war. Design decisions made expeditiously to accommodate unforeseen events favorably conspired to create the fastest combat aircraft of its era. But the Swallow's adolescence would prove to be a difficult one.

An unidentified Me 262 on display at Patterson Field in 1949. A V-1 buzz-bomb is located in the background. (Air Force Museum Collection)

The redesign of the BMW engine was originally not thought to be a serious setback to the Me 262's development timetable since the Jumo engines would be available shortly. But in November 1940 when the Jumo engine finally ran on the test stand, it was obvious that it too would not be available for flight testing any time soon. In February 1941 a decision was made to complete the first Me 262 prototype with two 1,653 LBF Walter (HWK) R II-203b rocket motors in lieu of the turbojets for initial flight testing. But these engines also ran into development problems, and the idea was soon dropped.

As a temporary measure, the first prototype (*Werk-Nr.* 262 000001, PC+UA) was fitted with a 750 hp Jumo 210Ga 12-cylinder liquid-cooled engine in the forward fuselage weapons bay and a wooden two-bladed propeller. This would allow some limited aerodynamic testing of the airframe to be accomplished pending the delivery of the jet engines. Construction of the **Me 262V1** began in January 1941 under the direction of Mortitz Asam in the Messerschmitt factory at Augsburg-Haunstetter. Initial flight tests would take place without the turbojet nacelles under the wings, although later flights would include these to evaluate their effects on aerodynamics.

Taxi tests were conducted at Augsburg on 17 April 1941, and the next day the Me 262V1 achieved 261 MPH on its first flight piloted by Messerschmitt Chief Test Pilot *Flugkapitän* Fritz Wendel. Because the wing was optimized for high-speed flight, coupled with the poor acceleration provided by the piston engine, Wendel needed every foot of the Augsburg runway to get airborne. The basic low-speed handling qualities of the aircraft were discovered to be satisfactory during the 18 minute flight, but minor buffeting and elevator oscillations were reported as speeds approached 335 MPH. Although the Me 262V1 was larger and heavier than the Bf 109, it was achieving slightly higher speeds, even though it was equipped with the same relatively underpowered piston engine. Messerschmitt believed this demonstrated that the basic Me 262 design was more aerodynamically efficient than contemporary German fighters.

The first prototype (Werks-Nr. 262 000001) shown with the Jumo 210Ga piston engine in the nose and without jet nacelles under the wings. The building in the background is the Messerschmitt Experimental Flight Test Building at Lager-Lechfeld. (Air Force Museum Collection)

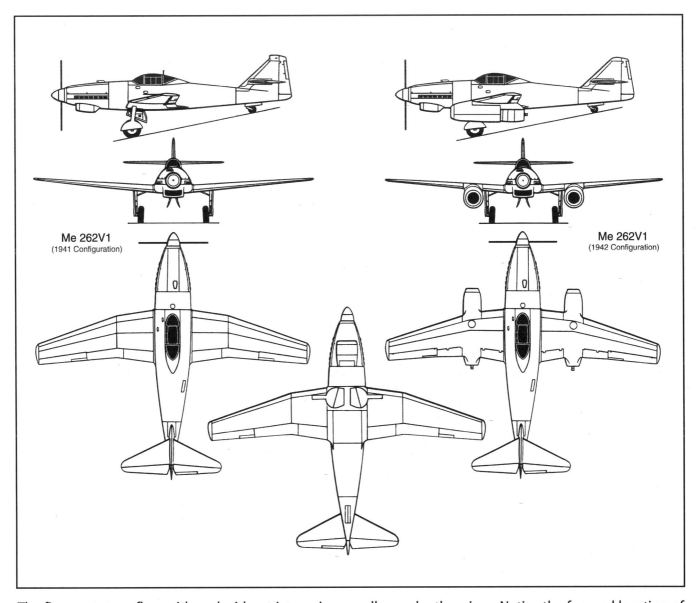

Me 262V1
(1941 Configuration)

Me 262V1
(1942 Configuration)

The first prototype flew with and without jet engine nacelles under the wings. Notice the forward location of the main landing gear, a featured shared with all the tail-dragger prototypes. Without the jet nacelles and the 'fillet' installed on the leading edge of the wing, it is hard to tell that this was a truly swept-wing aircraft. Also noteworthy is the slight evolution of the vertical stabilizer. Compare this to the vertical used on production aircraft. (Dennis R. Jenkins)

A total of 23 flights would be undertaken solely with the power of the Jumo 210Ga engine, the last being on 8 May 1941. In November 1941 a pair of pre-production BMW 003 engines finally arrived at Augsburg, each having been tested to a disappointingly low 1,015 LBF thrust. In February 1942 work commenced on fitting them into the nacelles on PC+UA and performing a number of static ground tests.

The prototype was finally cleared for flight testing, and the first flight of the Me 262 under jet power took place on 25 March 1942. It was just as well that the Jumo piston engine was still installed.

Shortly after take off, Wendel had reached an altitude of only 165 feet when first one, then both of the jets flamed out. With the added drag and weight of the two turbojets,

the Me 262V1 could barely remain airborne on the power of the Jumo 210Ga alone, but Wendel succeeded in completing a circuit of the airfield and landing safely. The engines were immediately removed by BMW personnel and it was discovered that the compressor blades in both engines had broken. Their failure was unexpected since the engines had run at higher loads in the test cell during tests at

18 July 1942. The third Me 262 prototype takes off for the first time under jet power. Pilot Fritz Wendel was not at all sure the aircraft would lift its tail sufficiently to get airborne, but a brief tap on the brakes proved to be the trick. (Air Force Museum Collection)

Berlin-Schönefeld. It was subsequently determined the BMW 003 needed to be completely redesigned, and the revised BMW 003A powerplant, with a greater mass flow and higher thrust, was not destined to fly until October 1943 beneath a Ju 88A test-bed. Further analysis showed that even if the engines had not failed, it was unlikely they would have operated satisfactorily since the propeller created too turbulent an airflow in front of the intakes. This may also have been a contributing factor in the failure of the compressor blades.

In the meantime, Jumo had succeeded in overcoming most of the problems of their engine. So the Me 262 design was modified to accommodate the Jumo 004 turbojet,

which by the end of 1941 had completed a successful ten-hour ground test and was developing 1,453 LBF thrust. However, during the summer of 1941 Jumo had been instructed by the RLM to redesign the 004A to minimize its usage of 'rationed materials,' primarily nickel and chromium. The design and dimensions of the new 004B engine would remain the same, but its construction techniques would be radically altered, much to its detriment.

The second and third prototype Me 262 airframes would be the first ones modified for the Jumo engines, which were somewhat larger and heavier than the BMW units. In order to accommodate the new engine, the nacelles had to be enlarged 10% in diameter and 16%

in length. This reshaping of the nacelles also dictated an increase in the area of the vertical stabilizer.

Due primarily to the fact that a paved runway was deemed desirable to eliminate possible foreign-object damage to the jet engines, the first jet-powered flight would take place at Leipheim, the location of all future Me 262 testing. Like Augsburg, the runway at nearby Leipheim was 3,600 feet long, although it was covered with tarmac instead of grass. The third prototype, **Me 262V3** (*Werk-Nr.* 262 000003, PC+UC), was the first Me 262 to fly on jet power alone, taking off from Leipheim on 18 July 1942 with two pre-production Jumo 004A-0 engines. Each of these engines provided 1,850 LBF thrust and, with a take-off weight of

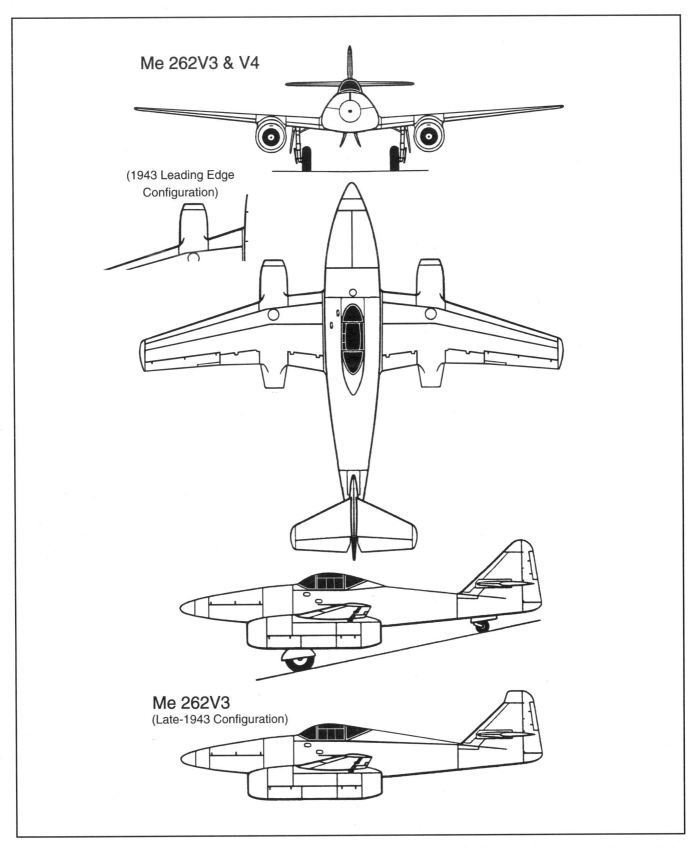

Me 262V3 & V4

(1943 Leading Edge Configuration)

Me 262V3
(Late-1943 Configuration)

The V3 and V4 were identical for most of their careers. Noteworthy is the lack of a mass balancer at the top of the rudder compared to production aircraft. The V3 was modified in late-1943 to test a more streamlined canopy and slightly different vertical stabilizer. Although this afforded a slight drag reduction, it was not adopted for production. (Dennis R. Jenkins)

The third prototype is refueled on 18 July 1942 between the two flights made on that day. The screens covering the jet intake is noteworthy. The open panel in the rear fuselage gives access to the push-pull control rods. Paint and markings are fairly typical for the early prototypes. (Air Force Museum Collection)

slightly more than 11,000 pounds, it was calculated the Me 262 should rotate at 112 MPH.

However, during high-speed taxi tests earlier in the day, Wendel reported that the elevators were proving ineffective at the calculated 112 MPH 'unstick' speed, and he could not raise the rear fuselage. Luckily, one of the observers on the field, aerodynamist Curt Zeiler, suggested that tapping the brakes at 112 MPH would tip the aircraft's nose forward, exposing the elevators to the air stream. The trick worked. The twelve minute flight began at 08:40 reaching an altitude of just over 6,000 feet and a speed of 375 MPH.

At five minutes past noon, Wendel took PC+UC on its second flight, tentatively exploring the handling characteristics of the aircraft. This flight lasted 13 minutes and reached 11,000 feet and 450 MPH. Various maneuvers were tried and minor problems uncovered, normal with any new aircraft, especially one so radical as the Me 262 was turning out to be. One of the problems was that in a bank the airflow broke away early from the wing center section, and after the flight it was decided to add a small fillet between the fuselage and engine nacelle, simultaneously increasing the root chord and continuing the leading-edge taper angle of the outer panels across the entire center section. At the same time, the leading-edge slots would be extended across the center section. This revised wing planform would first be tested in January 1943 on the Me 262V2, and would be retrofitted to all earlier prototypes except V1.

The first six flights of the Me 262V3 were made by Wendel with increasing confidence, and it was decided that an *Erprobungsstelle Rechlin* (test pilot school) representative should be allowed to fly the new aircraft. Therefore, the seventh flight was conducted by Henrich Beauvais on 11 August 1942, and it did not go exactly according to plan. Despite have been fully briefed by Wendel, Beauvais failed to get PC+UC airborne soon enough, and his left wing impacted an large, unfortunately placed, pile of manure in a field past the end of the runway. This sent the aircraft into a ground loop, severely damaging it, although Beauvais

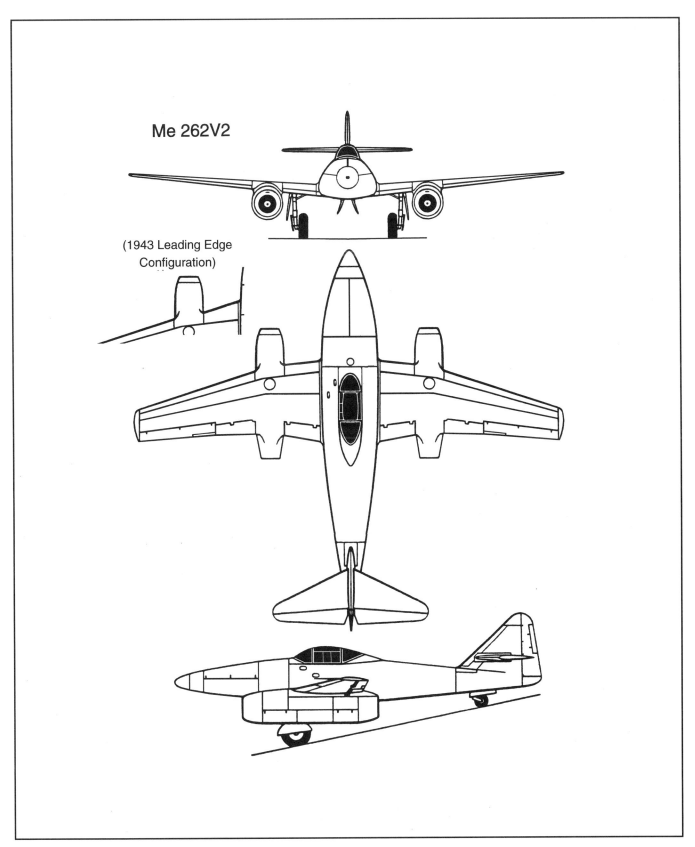

Me 262V2

(1943 Leading Edge
Configuration)

The first five prototypes used a different canopy than production aircraft. Notice the wrap-around front windscreen, and the framed side glass. A 'fillet' was installed on the leading edge of the inner wing during the test program, producing the final shape that is now so familiar. Compare the shape of the nose and vertical stabilizer with the production examples. (Dennis R. Jenkins)

The second prototype was the third aircraft to fly (the second on jet power). The tail-wheel undercarriage was discovered to be unsatisfactory since the wings blocked airflow to the horizontal stabilizers and there was no propeller-wash to make up for it. This led to an inability to lift the tail during the take-off run. The early canopy had a 'window' on the left side that could be opened, but proved difficult to seal when the cockpit was pressurized. Also note the relative position of the main landing gear compared to later nose-wheel equipped aircraft. (Air Force Museum Collection)

escaped serious injury. A post-accident investigation showed that high ambient air temperatures had degraded the performance of the Jumo engines more than predicted, and that Beauvais missed the appropriate moment to tap the brakes.

Although the airframe of the **Me 262V2** (*Werk-Nr.* 262 000002, PC+UB) was mostly complete by July 1941, its first flight did not occur until 1 October 1942, becoming the third Me 262 to fly. Subsequent flights were used primarily for performance and calibration tests. In January 1943, the small wing fillet found necessary after the first flight of Me 262V3 was installed between the fuselage and engine nacelle to produce a con-

stant sweepback on the entire leading edge. Although producing slightly more lift due to the greater area, the modification initially led to a vibration of the outer wing panel, resulting in a speed restriction of 430 MPH. The vibration was later cured, and all aircraft beginning with Me 262V5 were equipped with this wing planform.

During his tenure as *General der Jagdflieger* (General of the Fighter Forces), Ernst Udet had displayed little enthusiasm for jet aircraft, and had on several occasions even questioned their continued development. This attitude was initially maintained by Erhard Milch when he took over the post after Udet's suicide in November 1941. However, Milch could not ignore the

apparent success of the Me 262 flight test program, and shortly after the initial flights of the Me 262V2 he authorized the building of two additional prototypes (for a total of five flyable ones) and 15 pre-production examples. Nevertheless, Milch and the RLM both cautioned that they considered any preparation of series production to be premature. Although this decision was criticized after the war as crippling the Me 262 program, it should be remembered that there were only two jet-powered prototypes flying, and that the Jumo 004A-series engines were far from reliable powerplants that could carry an aircraft into combat. Nevertheless, the *Luftwaffe* decided to press ahead with the development of the Me 262 to the point it could

be placed in mass production if the need arose.

In January 1943, a specially prepared Me 262 fuselage, carried upside down under the starboard wing of the Me 323S9, was scheduled to be dropped into the Mürritzee to obtain information on the flutter characteristics of the tail surfaces. Since the Mürritzee had frozen over by 11 February 1943 when the tests were actually underway, it was decided to drop the fuselage from 20,000 feet over the Chiemsee. The tests were considered a failure since the recovery system did not function properly resulting in the loss of the fuselage and its data recorders. Later, on 23 October 1943 a second fuselage was dropped over Lake Constance to ascertain the terminal velocity of the airframe, although no conclusive data was obtained again due to a failure in the recovery system.

On 2 March 1943 the Me 262V1 finally took off under jet-only power (the third Me 262 to do so) fitted with Jumo 004A-0 engines. By this time the Jumo 210Ga had

been removed from the nose and replaced by three 30MM MG 151 cannon, and a partially pressurized cockpit had been added. On 7 July 1944, after 65 test flights, PC+UA was severely damaged during an emergency landing after a catastrophic engine failure. The airframe was considered a total loss and was not repaired.

After repairs following the Beauvais accident, the Me 262V3 flew again on 20 March 1943 at Lager-Lechfeld with *Hauptmann* Wolfgang Späte becoming the first operational *Luftwaffe* pilot to fly the type. Späte was highly impressed, even though his second flight resulted in a dual flame-out after he attempted a steep banking turn at 9,800 feet that disrupted the airflow to the engines. Luckily, Späte managed to restart the engines at 1,500 feet and land safely. Späte enthusiastically reported to *Oberkommando Luftwaffe* (Air Force High Command) that that the new aircraft was a quantum leap in performance over existing fighters.

Late in 1943 the fuselage of the

Me 262V3 was modified to extend the canopy fairing all the way to the vertical stabilizer in an attempt to reduce drag and solve the directional stability problem. The modification, reminiscent of the P-47 razorback design, provided a small decrease in drag, but did little to correct the basic instability problem. The aircraft was subsequently destroyed during an Allied air raid on 12 September 1944.

The Me 262V2 had made a total of 48 flights before being destroyed on 18 April 1943 in the first fatal accident of a Me 262. Test pilot Wilhelm Ostertag was killed when the aircraft impacted the ground following a high-speed dive near Hiltenfingen. The accident was apparently caused by a spontaneous change of horizontal stabilizer incidence, and was the first in what would be a series of similar accidents. Although the exact cause of the accidents was never discovered, the introduction of a different cockpit switch and a stronger electric actuator appeared to solve the problem.

A captured Me 262 adorned with an American stars-and-bars insignia. The fate of this aircraft is unknown, and it is possible it was scrapped prior to being returned to the United States. (Air Force Museum Collection)

PREMATURE PRODUCTION

THE ALLIES JOIN THE REVOLUTION

The fourth prototype **Me 262V4** (*Werk-Nr.* 262 000004, PC+UD) first flew on 15 May 1943 when *Flugkapitän* Fritz Wendel delivered the aircraft from Augsburg to Lager-Lechfeld. On 22 May 1943, at the urging of Wolfgang Späte who had flown the third prototype in March, *Generalleutnant* Adolf Galland visited Lager-Lechfeld and flew the Me 262V4. Galland was very impressed, and returned to Berlin to urge that the Me 262 receive a high priority and enter production immediately. Erhard Milch, in charge of *Luftwaffe* fighter production, accepted Galland's recommendation and agreed that the Me 209 would be superseded by the Me 262. A few days later Galland and Milch were informed that a British prisoner had witnessed a flight by a "… propellerless aircraft …" the previous Christmas. The *Luftwaffe* was not prepared to dismiss the possibility (a good thing, since the prototype Gloster E28/39 Meteor had begun flight tests in the summer of 1941), and this gave added impetus for placing the Me 262 into production.

But Galland agreed with Späte's assessment that the aircraft needed a substantial increase in endurance,

Unfortunately, not a terrific photograph, but interesting in that it shows the Me 262V10 (VI+AE) with a Deichselschlepp *towed-bomb. Also, under the fuselage near the wing trailing edge are two rocket-assisted take-off units. The prototypes generally carried their* Stammkennzeichen *alpha-numeric codes on their fuselage sides and the underside of their wings. (Air Force Museum Collection)*

The end of the line at Lager-Lechfeld. In the foreground is the Me 262V9, while V10 is at the extreme left. Various other test Me 262s litter the rest of the photo. Like most Me 262s captured at war's end, these have had their nose landing gear struts destroyed. (Air Force Museum Collection)

The second V7 was really Werk-Nr. 130303, and was later called V303. Noteworthy is the bomb pylon which shows up very well here. The angled black cartridge ejection chutes for the 30MM MK 108 cannon are just forward of the bomb pylon. The round opening in the extreme nose is the gun camera. (Air Force Museum Collection)

necessitating larger-capacity fuel tanks, which naturally led to an increase in take-off weight. In view of the techniques used to raise the tailplane during take-off, the *Luftwaffe* ordered that a nose-wheel undercarriage be fitted to the production model. Willy Messerschmitt was not particularly pleased at this recommendation, preferring to place the aircraft into production without modification, and to incorporate changes later in the production run. The *Luftwaffe* was insistent, and Messerschmitt eventually deferred to Galland's request.

At another production conference in Berlin, this one on 2 June 1943, the Me 262 was released for series production as a fighter. Production Program 223 was established with a goal of 60 Me 262s per month, and Milch was briefed on the production plans for the Me 262:

"... Construction of the wings, and final assembly, will take place at Augsburg, and construction of the fuselages and tails will take place at Regensburg. By concentrating our effort, and if certain suppositions are realized, we can have delivery of the first production aircraft by January 1944. Production will then rise in the second month to eight, in the third to 21, in April to 40, and in May to 60 aircraft. By the middle of May we shall reach the requested number of 100 aircraft and production will run at 60 aircraft per month ..."

In the meantime, despite the lack of test aircraft, every effort was being made by Messerschmitt to accelerate the development of the Me 262. The Me 309V3 was being utilized for development of an ejection seat and fully pressurized cockpit that were planned for the production Me 262. It should be noted

that neither item was actually incorporated into the production aircraft. And the Bf 109F-1 (*Werk-Nr.* 5603), which had previously participated in the Me 309 development program, had been employed to assist in the development of a suitable nose wheel arrangement.

The latter trials were continued with the **Me 262V5** (*Werk-Nr.* 262 000005, PC+UE) which was flown for the first time on 26 June 1943 with a fixed nose wheel taken from an Me 309. To correctly balance the aircraft, the main landing gear were moved approximately three feet aft.

Tricycle landing gear had been discussed even before the original P.1065 proposal had been submitted to the RLM. Messerschmitt and Voigt had decided against using it initially as they thought it added one more radical design departure

The clear vision canopy provided excellent visibility for the Me 262. The only armored glass was a 90MM thick piece on the front windscreen forcing a segmented windshield instead of the wrap-around plexiglass units used by the initial prototypes. (Jay Miller Collection via the Aerospace Education Center)

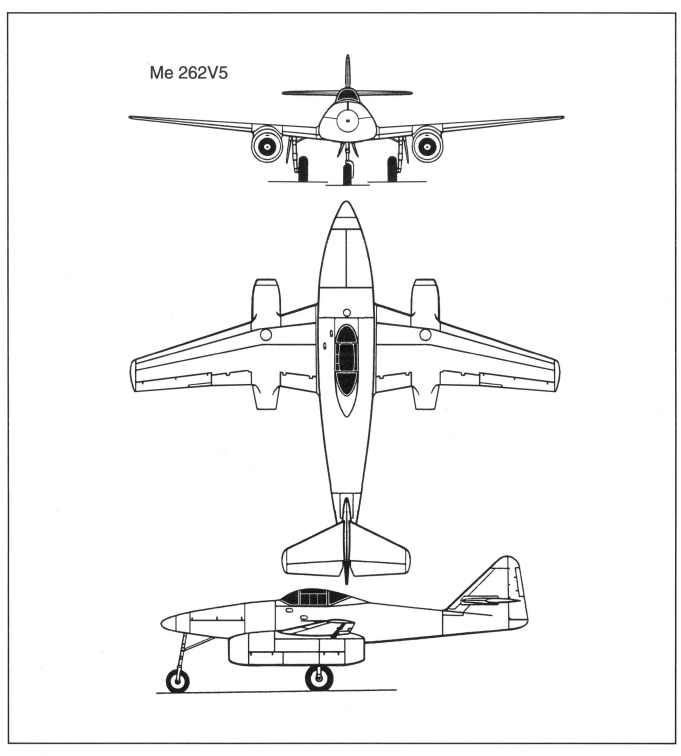

Me 262V5

The fifth prototype was the first equipped with a nose landing gear. The nose wheel was not retractable (notice the lack of landing gear doors), and the main gear doors were of a different configuration than production aircraft. (Dennis R. Jenkins)

(in addition to jet engines and swept wings) and therefore increased the development risk. The *Luftwaffe* insisted however, especially after the near tragic flight of Henrich Beauvais in PC+UC. The nose gear would prove to be fragile, and a number of aircraft suffered accidents during landings when the nose gear collapsed. The nose gear was also intolerant of some ground-towing techniques, leading to more failures. However, this problem has been exaggerated in many books since photographs taken immediately after the war show numerous Me 262s with collapsed nose gears. In reality most of these were the result of the Germans sabotaging the aircraft to prevent the Allies from using them. The most expedient way to accomplish this was a hand grenade attached to the nose strut.

Although the aircraft was easier to control during take-off, and no longer needed a tap on the brakes to raise the tail, initial tests showed no significant increase in take-off performance. It was subsequently decided to use this aircraft for tests involving two Borsig RI 502 take-off assistance rockets, each providing 1,100 LBF thrust for six seconds. Initial trials were conducted by Karl Baur. with the rockets mounted beneath the fuselage immediately aft of the center-of-gravity. During the first take-off, Baur ignited the rockets at approximately 100 MPH, and the nose wheel immediately left the ground, necessitating the application of full forward stick to prevent the aircraft from taking-off before sufficient airspeed had been achieved to remain flying. For subsequent tests, the thrust line of the rockets was made more horizontal, with somewhat greater success, and the rockets reduced the take-off roll of the aircraft by approximately 900 feet. Later, a pair of 2,205 LBF thrust rockets were tested, and it was determined that the Me 262V5 could take off in less than 1,300 feet.

The summer and fall of 1943 was not a good time for the Me 262 prototypes. On 25 July 1943, the Me 262V4 was successfully demonstrated for Hermann Göring at Rechlin piloted by Gerd Lindner. However, the next day, PC+UD crashed while taking off from Schkeuditz on its 51st flight. Gerd Lindner was at the controls, and although he escaped serious injury, the aircraft was considered a total loss. And on 4 August 1943, while on its 74th flight, the Me 262V5 was damaged as a result of nose gear failure. After completion of repairs, the aircraft crashed again on 1 February 1944 at Lager-Lechfeld after suffering a nose wheel tire blow-out while being flown by *Hauptmann* Werner Thierfelder, and although reparable, this had not been accomplished prior to the end of the war.

Following its first flight on 17 October 1943, the **Me 262V6** (*Werk-Nr.* 130001, VI+AA) joined the flight test fleet. Due to the complex nature of the Me 262 test program, and the number of prototypes that had been lost or damaged, it was decided to allocate the pre-production aircraft *Versuchs* numbers. This

Unusual for a captured Me 262 ... the nose gear has not been blown up by the Germans. This mostly completed aircraft was captured at one of the 'forest factories' where most Me 262s were manufactured. (Air Force Museum Collection)

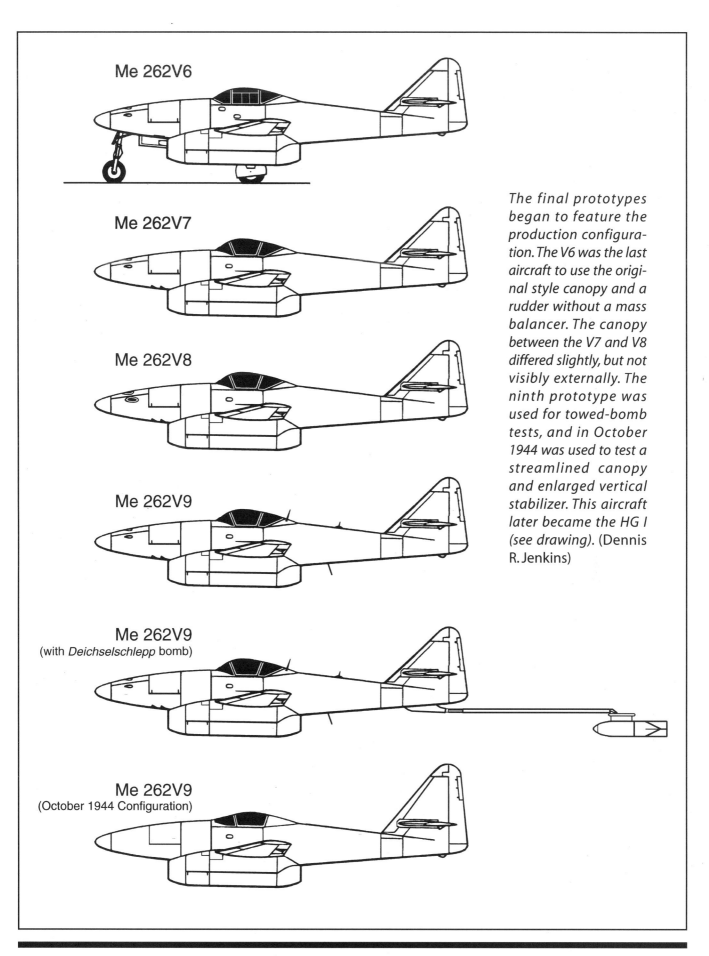

Me 262V6

Me 262V7

Me 262V8

Me 262V9

Me 262V9
(with *Deichselschlepp* bomb)

Me 262V9
(October 1944 Configuration)

The final prototypes began to feature the production configuration. The V6 was the last aircraft to use the original style canopy and a rudder without a mass balancer. The canopy between the V7 and V8 differed slightly, but not visibly externally. The ninth prototype was used for towed-bomb tests, and in October 1944 was used to test a streamlined canopy and enlarged vertical stabilizer. This aircraft later became the HG I (see drawing). (Dennis R. Jenkins)

aircraft was powered by two pre-production Jumo 004B-0 turbojets, each weighing 220 pounds less than the 004A while still delivering 1,980 LBF thrust. The turbojets were housed in redesigned low-drag nacelles, the fairing panel from the trailing edge of the wing being carried down to enclose the rear of the engine in order to improve the airflow characteristics. Some cooling problems had been observed during early test flights, and it had been decided to increase the flow of air over the rear section of the engine by introducing a series of slots radially in the external section of the double skinning, the metal in front of each slot being slightly depressed to form a shallow scoop.

In addition, external elevator balances were fitted, and gun ports were provided in the nose, although no weapons were installed. The ejector chutes for spent shell casings located on the bottom-sides of the fuselage were a different configuration that that of later aircraft. The most significant change from earlier aircraft was the provision of a fully-retractable, hydraulically-operated tricycle undercarriage. The aircraft was used to open the Me 262's maneuvering envelope but on 9 March 1944 the Me 262V6 crashed during its 28th flight, killing pilot Kurt Schmidt.

It was during this time that the Me 262's fate took a turn that a few historians believe could have influenced the outcome of the war. On 2 November 1943, Hermann Göring and Erhard Milch visited the Messerschmitt

The final assembly line at Obertraubling 'forest factory' near Regensburg Germany after an Allied bombing attack. The camouflage netting covering the build-up area can be seen in the background. Various subassemblies were built-up at remote sites scattered around the surrounding forests, then brought together on this final assembly line. The aircraft would be checked out at the end of the line, then towed to a nearby Autobahn that was used as a runway. These aircraft were basically complete, including engines when they were destroyed. (Air Force Museum Collection)

WARBIRD**TECH**
SERIES

The Me 262's flaps were extremely simple with interconnected segments on either side of the Jumo 004. Here the nacelle has been removed, but the engine is still attached to the wing. The Zwiebel exhaust cone is clearly visible in its retracted position. (Air Force Museum Collection)

The Air Force Museum's aircraft after restoration. Today this aircraft resides inside the main museum building, well protected from the elements. Most all subassemblies are still with the aircraft, the cockpit is mostly complete, as are the fuel tanks and various radios and other equipment, although the aircraft is not in flyable condition. (Air Force Museum Collection)

A completely outfitted nose section is ready to be attached to the forward fuselage. The nose landing gear has not been attached yet. (Air Force Museum Collection)

The trailing edge flaps were split around the engine nacelle, which is missing in this photo. The Frise-type ailerons are also missing. This is the Air Force Museum's Me 262A-1a undergoing restoration. (Air Force Museum Collection)

works at Augsburg to discuss the production of the Me 262. Göring asked Willy Messerschmitt if the Me 262 was capable of carrying bombs and Messerschmitt responded that the aircraft had been designed from the outset with provisions for carrying small (551 or 1,102-pound) weapons under the fuselage.

Arrangements were made for a demonstration of the latest combat aircraft before Göring and Adolf Hitler at Insterburg, Prussia, on 26 November 1943. Despite the urgency placed on the Me 262 program, preparations were made to display the aircraft for Hitler and the Me 262V4 and V6 were withdrawn from test duties and sent to Insterburg, flown by Karl Baur and Gerd Lindner. The Me 262V4 flown by Baur suffered a flame-out during take-off, but the Me 262V6 was demonstrated by Lindner with considerable effect. Hitler questioned Messerschmitt on the aircraft's ability to carry bombs, and Messerschmitt explained that this was possible with minimal modifications. Hitler was greatly impressed, and proclaimed that he had finally found his *Blitz-Bomber*.

From this point onward, the Me 262 featured prominently in Hitler's counter-invasion plans. Hitler was sure that a fast aircraft, with the ability to deliver even minimal quantities of bombs, could pin-down the invaders long enough to transfer reserve forces into the area. Unfortunately, Messerschmitt had not even begun work on a proto-type bomb-carrying Me 262.

During the course of November 1943, the second pre-production aircraft (*Werk-Nr.* 130002, VI+AB) had been rolled-out of the Augsburg, and the **Me 262V7** made its

first flight on 20 December 1943 piloted by Gerd Lindner. This was similar to its immediate predecessor except in having a clear-vision blown canopy and a rubber-sealed pressurized cabin affording a pressure ratio of 1:2 (*e.g.*; an pressure equivalent to 20,000 feet was maintained at an altitude of 40,000 feet). The clear-vision canopy substituted an armored three-segment windscreen for the single-piece wraparound windscreen on earlier prototypes, and eliminated the 'window' on the left side of the main canopy. Production specification Jumo 004B-1 engines were fitted for the first time although they differed little from the pre-production units. On 21 February 1944 the aircraft was damaged in the course of its 17th flight. The Me 262V7 was repaired, but after a total of 13 flight hours the aircraft was totally destroyed in a crash at Lager-Lechfeld on 19 May 1944, killing pilot *Unteroffizier* Hans Flachs.

The Allies' first photographic evidence of the Me 262 had come in January 1943 when the RAF discovered an Me 262 on the field at Augsburg, and by December 1943 Allied intelligence was beginning to obtain hard data on the Me 262 design. On at least two separate occasions, French citizens employed at the Messerschmitt factory managed to escape with information concerning the Me 262, as well as the Me 163 and He 280. This data prompted the RAF to order 120 Gloster Meteor fighters into production, as well as initiating investigations to better understand the aerodynamic problems associated with transonic and supersonic flight. Similar programs were undertaken in the United States, culminating in the Bell P-59A, Lockheed P-80A, and the experimental

Bell XS-1 (X-1).

The fourth pre-production aircraft, **Me 262V9** (*Werk-Nr.* 130004, VI+AD), made its first flight on 19 January 1944 and was initially used to test communication equipment. Like VI+AB, this aircraft was powered by production Jumo 004B-1 engines. Me 262V9 was also used to test such novel concepts as an electro-acoustical homing device which operated through small antenna located around the nose. During October 1944 VI+AD was

The vertical stabilizer of Werk-Nr. *111711 during evaluation at Wright Field.* (Air Force Museum Collection)

The entire horizontal stabilizer could be adjusted for incidence by an electrically-driven screw jack bolted to the front face of the slanting fin spar. The failure of this screw jack resulted in the loss of several early Me 262s. (Air Force Museum Collection)

The front (main) wing spar. The cockpit liner can be seen directly above it, and the main landing gear doors are at the bottom of the photo. (Air Force Museum Collection)

modified with a streamlined *Rennkabine* (racing) canopy and enlarged vertical stabilizer as a high-performance testbed. The aircraft made at least 20 flights in this configuration, and was later used by the Oberammergau Project Bureau for further high-speed research leading to the *Hochgeschwindikeit* series of high-speed aircraft.

Erhard Milch fully acknowledged the importance of the *Blitz-Bomber* concept, but seemingly ignoring Hitler's orders, endeavored to produce the Me 262 as a fighter. This role was highlighted when the **Me 262V8** (*Werk-Nr.* 130003, VI+AC) made its first flight on 13 March 1944. VI+AC carried four Rheinmetall-Borsig 30mm MK 108 cannon fitted in the nose and a *Revi* 16B optical gunsight installed in the cockpit. These were considered effective air-to-air weapons, but were almost useless against ground targets. Each MK 108 could fire 660

rounds of 0.75-pound high-explosive shells per minute and were considered nearly ideal ballistically. Some difficulties were experienced during flight tests when the weapons were fired in a turn, centrifugal forces tearing the ammunition belts, and this was partially rectified by changing the feed mechanism, although jamming would continue to plague the Me 262 during its brief operational career. Fire from the four weapons converged at 450–500 yards, and the two upper weapons were provided with 100 rounds each, while the lower two had 80 rounds each. The Me 262V8 was soon fitted with a slightly reshaped cockpit canopy in an effort to eliminate some distortion problems introduced on the Me 262V7. The aircraft was destroyed in a landing accident in October 1944.

Milch's desire to produce the Me 262 as a fighter was undoubtedly influenced by intelligence he was receiving on the new Boeing B-29 and Convair B-32 long-range heavy bombers being developed in the United States. According to his intelligence, the aircraft had a combat ceiling of up to 39,000 feet, rendering all of the *Luftwaffe's* fighters useless—all except the Me 262. Milch believed if he did not produce sufficient fighters to destroy these bombers, then Ger-

many had surely lost the war. As it turned out, the combat ceiling of the B-29 was no where near 39,000 feet, and the aircraft would never fly operational missions in the European theater. But Milch had no way of knowing this.

Meanwhile, on 8 January 1944,

the first prototype of the Lockheed P-80 Shooting Star was flown by test pilot Milo Bircham. Three months earlier, on 23 September 1943, Geoffrey de Havilland Jr. had taken the prototype de Havilland Vampire into the air on its maiden flight. The Me 262's chance for glory was rapidly fading.

The Me 262 cockpit was simplistic by today's standards, but thoroughly adequate in its day. Instrumentation was basic, with flight instruments to the left on the main panel, and engine instruments to the right. The slanted side panel contained oxygen controls and gauges, plus emergency flap and landing gear controls. (Air Force Museum Collection)

FLEDGLING 4 SWALLOWS

AN ADOLESCENT GOES TO WAR

By January 1944, 23 additional airframes had been completed but could not be flown due to a lack of engines. Junkers was having a great deal of difficulty mass producing the Jumo 004 and the Ar 234 was also competing with the Me 262 for the meager supply of engines that were available. Had the pre-production airframes been completed earlier they would merely have had to wait longer to receive engines. Thus, had the *Generalluftzeugmeister Amt* exercised less caution and ordered the Me 262 into mass production at an earlier date, it would not have materially affected the issue.

Junkers had been opposed to rushing the Jumo 004B into production as numerous technical problems still needed to be resolved before the engine could be considered a reliable powerplant. Only a trickle of Jumo 004Bs were manufactured through June 1944 when, although still considered insufficiently developed, the design was 'frozen' for mass production. The situation was aggravated by the need to move production of the turbojet underground.

One of the major problems was that Junkers was having to produce a very state-of-the-art engine without the proper materials. Ideally, nickel and chromium would have been used extensively in the high-temperature areas of the engine. However, these materials were in short supply in Germany, and substitute materials had been pressed into service when the 004A had been redesigned into the 004B. For example, the combustion chambers were made out of ordinary steel with a spray coating of aluminum for heat resistance, resulting in frequent failures. The early production engines had a service life of less than ten hours, and were very unforgiving of the pilots that controlled it. The compression flow had a tendency to break down at moderate speeds and high altitudes, resulting in compressor stalls. The fuel flow was also

Eight Me 262s of Erprobungskommando 262 *lined up at Lager-Lechfeld. In addition of yellow numbers painted on the nose, EKdo 262 used a yellow band painted around the fuselage forward of the national cross. The* Werk-Nr. *is painted in black just above the horizontal stabilizer. (Air Force Museum Collection)*

extremely difficult to regulate, the turbine burning out if the fuel was admitted too quickly, and flaming-out if admitted too slowly. More than any other single factor, the difficulties in getting reliable engines limited the Me 262's effectiveness in 1944.

The last aircraft to be completed at Augsburg-Haunstetten, the **Me 262V10** (*Werk-Nr.* 130005, VI+AE), first flew on 15 April 1944. The long delay between the the first flight of Me 262V9 and Me 262V10 was simple—there were no engines. The Me 262V10 was initially used to evaluate means of reducing control stick forces since these became unacceptably heavy at high speeds. The first Me 262 ailerons had a fairly well-rounded raised leading edge with the hinge set well back, and attempts were made to reduce their heaviness by first increasing and then reducing the profile. This was unsuccessful, and a blunt leading edge was tested with the hinge set further aft. The aileron shroud gap was varied and a geared tab arrangement was also tried, but even in the form finally adopted for production the ailerons were too heavy at high speeds.

The Me 262V10 was therefore fitted with a 'gear change' control col-

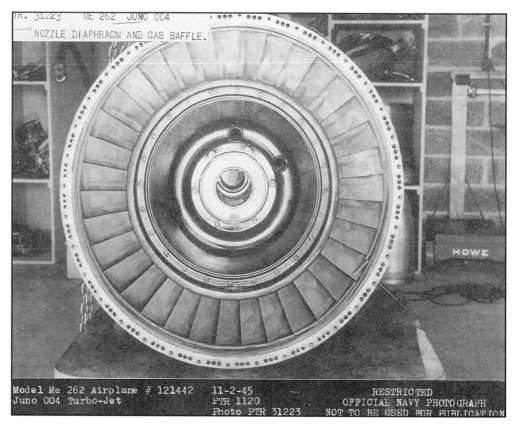

NOZZLE DIAPHRAGM AND GAS BAFFLE.

Model Me 262 Airplane # 121442   11-2-45   RESTRICTED
Juno 004 Turbo-Jet   PTR 1120   OFFICIAL NAVY PHOTOGRAPH
                            Photo PTR 31223 NOT TO BE USED FOR PUBLICATION

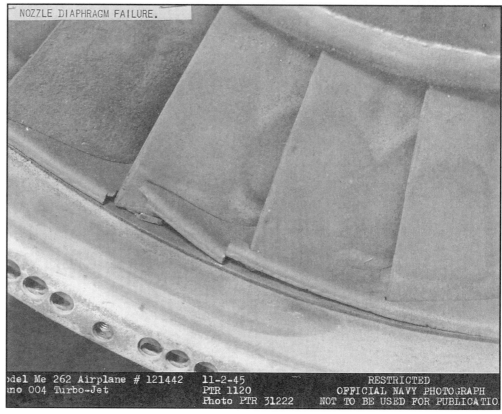

NOZZLE DIAPHRAGM FAILURE.

Model Me 262 Airplane # 121442   11-2-45   RESTRICTED
Juno 004 Turbo-Jet   PTR 1120   OFFICIAL NAVY PHOTOGRAPH
                            Photo PTR 31222 NOT TO BE USED FOR PUBLICATIO

One of the compressor blades in this captured Jumo 004B engine failed, although it did not result in the destruction of the compressor. The broken blade is located at the lower right (at about the 4-o'clock position) on the compressor. (Air Force Museum Collection)

umn so that the mechanical advantage could be changed by the pilot when he needed to maneuver at high speeds. The column consisted of a cylindrical sleeve and a stick which slid up and down within the sleeve. The sleeve was permanently fixed at a ball and socket in the floor of the cockpit, and the control rods were attached to the lower extremity of the stick. By means of a hand crank on the side of the sleeve, the stick could be raised at high speeds, and through an increase in leverage, reduce the stick forces. Full extension of the stick reduced aileron throw from 22 to 18 degrees.

As a result of the engine shortages, deliveries to the *Luftwaffe* did not begin until April 1944. A total of sixteen pre-production Me 262A-0 fighters were received in April, but only seven in May. On 28 March 1944, the first aircraft to come off the Leipheim production line (*Werk-Nr.* 130007, VI+AG) made its initial flight. The losses among the prototypes and the priority assigned to testing resulted in the **Me 262S1** being assigned to flight testing. On 25 June 1944 *Feldwebel* Herlitzius attained a speed of 624 MPH (1,004 KPH) in a steep power-dive from 23,000 feet while flying VI+AG. This was the first recorded

instance of any aircraft intentionally exceeding 1,000 KPH. The next two S-series aircraft (130008, VI+AH and 130009, VI+AI) were finally allocated to the *Luftwaffe*, and sent to *Erprobungskommando Thierfelder* (Fighter Test Detachment). The fourth Leipheim-built aircraft (*Werk-Nr.* 130010, VI+AJ) was sent to Blöhm und Voss' Wenzendorf factory for conversion into a two-seat trainer. The aircraft was delivered to the test detachment based at Rechlin-Lärz at the end of July 1944, but was written-off following a crash while landing on its 47th flight on 8 October 1944.

Model Me-262 Airplane # 121442   11-1-45   RESTRICTED
Juno 004 Turbo-Jet   PTR 1120   OFFICIAL NAVY PHOTOGRAPH
                                   Photo PTR 31211 NOT TO BE USED FOR PUBLICATION

The beautiful work produced by Junkers is obvious in this photo of the turbine section of a Jumo 004B. Unfortunately, the engine did not function as beautifully as it looked due to the materials available to produce it. (Air Force Museum Collection)

WARBIRD**TECH**
S E R I E S

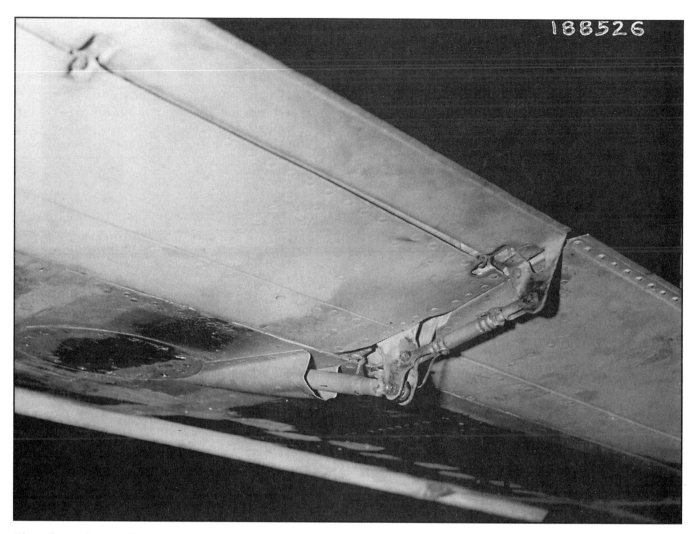

The aileron hinge of the Me 262 was mounted externally on the bottom of the wing. Auxiliary linkage adjustable only on the ground controlled the trim tab. (Air Force Museum Collection)

Sufficient numbers of Me 262A-0 fighters were also available to form a service trials unit, and the *Erprobungskommandos 262* (Proving Detachment) was established. Gradually, the pilots of *EKdo 262* began to gain experience with the new fighter and its temperamental engines. They also began to appreciate the enormous advantage its tremendous performance gave them in combat. With a maximum usable speed in excess of 540 MPH and an initial rate of climb of almost 4,000 feet per minute, the Me 262 outperformed every other aircraft in the sky. Moreover, the four 30MM cannon could discharge 99 pounds of high explosives in a three second burst, causing serious damage to bomber formations.

The aircraft had arrived at exactly the right moment, or so it seemed. By the spring of 1944, American P-51 Mustangs had begun escorting the bomber formations over Germany. The Mustang was more than equal to any conventional *Luftwaffe* fighter, and had the range to accompany the bombers all the way to their targets and home. This was an unfortunate development for the *Luftwaffe*—their fighters could carry the heavy armament necessary to kill the bombers, but then they could not maneuver with the P-51s; or they could carry light armament and maneuver with the Mustangs, but lack sufficient firepower to inflict much damage on the bombers. The exception to this was the Me 262, which carried heavier armament than any other contemporary fighter, and had the speed to simply avoid the Mustangs.

Despite the fact that Hitler's desire to use the Me 262 as a fighter-bomber was incomprehensible to the manufacturer, both conventional and unconventional means of adapting the aircraft for this role were finally being investigated during the early months of 1944. The conventional approach entailed installing a pair of bomb pylons side-by-side beneath the fuselage nose, forward of the main landing gear wells. Possible loads included two 551-pound bombs, or two 1,102-pound bombs. Alternately, a single 2,205-pound bomb could be carried, but in practice a single 1,102-pound or a pair of 551-pound bombs were normally carried.

The unconventional approach was provided by a *Deichselschlepp* (pole-tow) bomb—a 2,205-pound or 1,102-pound bomb fitted with a wooded wing (taken from a V1 buzz-bomb) and towed by means of a 20-foot tube rigidly attached to the bomb. The tow-bar was attached beneath the tail of the Me 262 by means of a swivel joint permitting horizontal and vertical motion. Wires to detonate the explosive bolts which attached the wings to the bomb passed through the tube. A two-wheeled dolly was fitted to the bomb during take-off and was jettisoned by means of an explosive bolt once the aircraft and bomb were airborne. The Me 262 was put into a shallow dive upon reaching the target, and aimed the bomb using normal *Revi* gunsight.

The Me 262V10 flown by Gerd Lindner was the first aircraft to be utilized for towed-bomb tests. With the bomb on tow, the speed of the Me 262 was reduced to some 320-330 MPH, and while experiments with the 1,102 pound bomb were satisfactory, difficulties were encountered when towing the 2,205 pound bomb because the auxiliary wing provided too high a lift coefficient. This caused the bomb to porpoise and the motion was transmitted to the Me 262, causing significant control problems. During one flight, Lindner was forced to bail out owing to the uncontrollable motion of the aircraft and the inability to jettison

The interior of the aft fuselage, from the production joint looking aft. The control linkages for the tail surfaces can be seen to the right, while the compass is on the bottom at center. A shelf to the left will eventually hold the radios. (Air Force Museum Collection)

The underside of the wing without the engine nacelle attached. The wingtip is to the left, and the leading edge is at the top. A panel has been removed to allow access to fuel and hydraulic plumbing. (Air Force Museum Collection)

the bomb. Tests were continued with a pre-production Me 262A-0, and on one occasion the explosive bolts failed to function and Lindner was forced to land the aircraft with the bomb still attached to the towbar. Yet another test terminated when the towing swivel wrenched itself out of the tail of the Me 262 as a result of too tight a turn. Eventually it was concluded that the towed bomb concept was too hazardous, and that more conventional methods of transporting bombs were preferable. But the concept would be reborn later to carry additional fuel for an advanced night-fighter variant.

The discussion of the Me 262's fighter-bomber role was opened again on 23 May 1944 when Hitler summoned Göring, Milch, Galland, and other senior officers to Berlin to review the latest *Luftwaffe* production plans. During the meeting Hitler listened to the discussion concerning Me 262 fighter production, but interrupted to ask how many fighter-bomber versions had been produced. When told that production had concentrated solely on the fighter version, Hitler lost his composure. His mood did not improve when informed that the fighter version was incapable of carrying even small bombs. Not only was he bitterly disappointed

at the loss of one of his most important anti-invasion weapons, Hitler was extremely angry at having been deliberately misled about the ability of production Me 262s to carry bombs.

The result was that Hitler made Göring personally responsible for the rapid production of a fighter-bomber Me 262, regardless of the effect this would have on the fighter version. Göring told Milch that the *Führer* had ordered the Me 262 to enter service exclusively as a fighter-bomber, and that all work on fighter variants was to be discontinued. The next day Göring discussed the modifications necessary to convert the Me 262 into a fighter-bomber with senior *Luftwaffe* officers. These changes could be included in new-production aircraft relatively easily, but modifying already built airframes would be extremely difficult. The level of difficulty did not matter. Once during the course of the subsequent conversation, Willy Messerschmitt inadvertently referred to the Me 262 as a fighter and was interrupted immediately by Göring who requested that he should stop using the term 'fighter.' The *Reichsmarschall*, obviously afraid of incurring Hitler's wrath, almost begged those present to do nothing behind his back that might upset the *Führer*'s wishes. A few days later Hitler partly relented, and agreed to allow continued testing of fighter variants as long as they did not impact the fighter-bomber program.

But for all the politics, the fact remained—the limiting factor in the production of the Me 262 was not determining its role, but figuring out how to mass produce the Jumo 004. When Allied troops came ashore at Normandy on 6 June, just ten days after the stormy conference with Hitler, less than 30 Me 262s had been delivered to operational *Luftwaffe* units.

When the original fighter aircraft finally reached combat units, hasty modifications were incorporated to turn them into fighter-bombers. Extra fuel tanks were fitted, 55 gallons beneath the pilot's seat, and another 130 gallons behind the existing rear tank. The latter, far aft of the normal center-of-gravity, made the aircraft extremely tail-heavy and almost impossible to fly if not counter-balanced. This was achieved by the addition of two 551-pound bombs beneath the fuselage at the wing leading edge, and the removal of two of the four 30MM cannon. It was vital that the rear-most fuel tank be emptied first to balance the aircraft in flight since dropping the bombs prior to emptying the aft fuel tank generally had disastrous results.

There were other problems. Because the Me 262 was aerodynamically very clean, it built up speed in dives very rapidly. This made it unsuitable for typical *Luftwaffe* steep-diving attacks (as exemplified by the *Stuka*). And because the pilot was unable to see directly below and ahead of the aircraft to aim his bombs, horizontal attacks from medium and high altitudes proved to be very ineffective.

The main landing gear strut on the starboard side. Some aircraft did not use conventional cast/forged and machined pieces, instead relying on drawn seamless tubing for primary structure. The large tread blocks on the main tires are noteworthy since the Me 262 was designed to operate from unpaved airfields. (Air Force Museum Collection)

For all of its many limitations, the Me 262 now fulfilled Hitler's requirements for an anti-invasion *Blitz-Bomber*. By now, however, even Hitler acknowledged the aircraft was unsuited to the role, and ordered the production of the jet-powered Arado Ar 234 light bomber to be accelerated.

On 26 July 1944, *Leutnant* Alfred Schreiber from *Kommando Thierfelder* shot down an RAF Mosquito reconnaissance aircraft while flying the **Me 262S12** (*Werk-Nr.* 130017, VI+AQ). It is the first aerial victory by a jet fighter in aviation history. On 18 July 1944 Werner Thierfelder was killed when the **Me 262S6** (*Werk-Nr.* 130011, VI+AK) crashed near Landsberg. An investigation later determined that a catastrophic separation of the turbine stator rings as the likely cause.

According to Messerschmitt records a total of 10 prototypes and 112 production aircraft had been manufactured by 10 August 1944. The 1st, 2nd, 4th, 5th, 6th, and 7th prototypes had been lost, 21 production aircraft had been destroyed by Allied bombing of the factories, and a further 11 had been lost due to accidents. The remaining aircraft were assigned to:

I.Gruppe of *Kampfgeschwader (KG) 51*; fighter-bombers; 33

Erprobungskommandos (EKdo) 262; fighters; 15

Rechlin Test Center; varied; 14

The main landing gear wells actually protruded through the tops of the wing structure, leading to the triangular-shaped fuselage on the Me 262. No extension hydraulics or uplocks were provided on the main landing gear. Instead, the wheels rested on the gear doors, which were locked into place. When the pilot wanted to lower the landing gear, he unlocked the doors, and gravity lowered the landing gear. (Air Force Museum Collection)

Retained at Messerschmitt for testing; varied; 11

Retained at Junkers for engine testing; fighter; 1

At Blöhm & Voss for conversion to two-seaters; fighter; 10

On 28 August 1944, USAAF Major Joseph Myers and Lieutenant M. D. Croy, Jr., both flying Republic P-47s from the 82nd Fighter Squadron, are credited with the first confirmed Me 262 kill—an Me 262A-1a from *Kampfgeschwader 51*.

A month after his appointment as the Chief of the General Staff, *Generalleutnant* Werner Kreipe attempted to bring pressure to bear on the *Führer* to increase home air defense in general and to reverse his decision to employ the Me 262 for bombing. On 30 August 1944 he succeeded in obtaining a minor concession from Hitler—every 20th Me 262 could be delivered as a fighter. Kreipe believed this was unsatisfactory, and after a heated argument with Hitler, submitted his resignation on 19 September. Nevertheless, on 4 November Hitler finally gave his permission for production of the Me 262 as a fighter, but even then he stipulated that each aircraft "… must be able to carry at least one 551-pound bomb in case of emergency." This stipulation was tacitly ignored.

During the final three months of 1944, a total of 350 Me 262s were manufactured, finally giving sufficient numbers for the aircraft to be deployed in roles other than as a fighter-bomber. In November, *Kommando Welter*

The Me 262 nose gear was a study in simplicity. Unlike the main gear, however, it was equipped with hydraulics for both retraction and extension. The nose gear proved to be a weak point in the Me 262 design, and it frequently collapsed when treated too harshly by inexperienced pilots. (Air Force Museum Collection)

was formed to fly Me 262B-1a/U1 night-fighter variants. The initial aircraft assigned to the unit were ordinary single-seat Me 262 fighters, although one of them had been modified into the Me 262A-1a/U2 with a pilot-operated FuG 218 *Neptun* radar. The first targets for the new night fighters were the fast-flying Mosquito bombers of the Royal Air Force, which until now had flown with relative impunity. Around the same time, *Kommando Braunegg* was formed as a short-range reconnaissance group flying Me 262A-1a/U3s that were basically fighter models with camera equipment installed instead of the normal 30MM cannon.

The Me 262 continued to suffer from yawing motions at high speeds, and two aircraft were assigned to a flight test program in an attempt to find a cure. *Werk-Nr.* 170056 (V056) and *Werk-Nr.* 130167 (V167) tested various modifications aimed at improving lateral stability. V056 participated in a test series where varying amounts of the vertical stabilizer were removed, and on the final test, only about 12-inches of the fin were left in place. This test series also included the addition of a small vertical stabilizer to the forward fuselage of V167.

The starboard leading edge slots in the extended position. The engine nacelle is missing. The slots were manufactured from sheet steel since it was readily available and easy to manufacture. (Air Force Museum Collection)

The starboard leading edge slots in the retracted position. The slots were fully automatic in the operation, the position being determined simply by aerodynamic forces upon the wing. (Air Force Museum Collection)

MESSERSCHMITT
Me 262 STURMVOGEL

43

SCHWALBE ÜND 5 STURMVOGEL

PRODUCTION SWALLOWS CONFRONT THE ALLIES

Unofficially called *Schwalbe* (Swallow), the first production variant was the **Me 262A-1a** single-seat interceptor fighter and was essentially identical to late pre-production Me 262A-0 fighters. It entered service with *Erprobungskommandos (EKdo) 262* at Lager-Lechfeld in July 1944. The **Me 262A-1a/Jabo** was an unofficial designation given to Me 262A-1a aircraft converted in the field for the *Blitz-Bomber* role by adding bomb pylons and bomb fusing equipment.

The Me 262A-1a was considered easier to fly than the Bf 109G in many respects. However, because of the wide range of speeds at which it was intended to operate, its design was something of a compromise. Although it could not turn as tightly as its piston-engined contemporaries, it could hold its speed in tight turns for much longer than conventional fighters. Since the turbojets took time to spool, acceleration and deceleration were accomplished relatively more slowly than with propeller-driven aircraft, but the Me 262A-1a could dive extremely rapidly, and care had to be taken not to exceed its critical Mach number. During climbs and turns the automatic leading-edge

Me 262A-1a Werk-Nr. 500079 (F1+DA) from Stab/KG 76 at Giebelstadt after its capture. The aircraft had apparently suffered minor damage after the collapse of its left main landing gear. The torque-tube that supported the top of the nose section is visible in the access space. (Air Force Museum Collection)

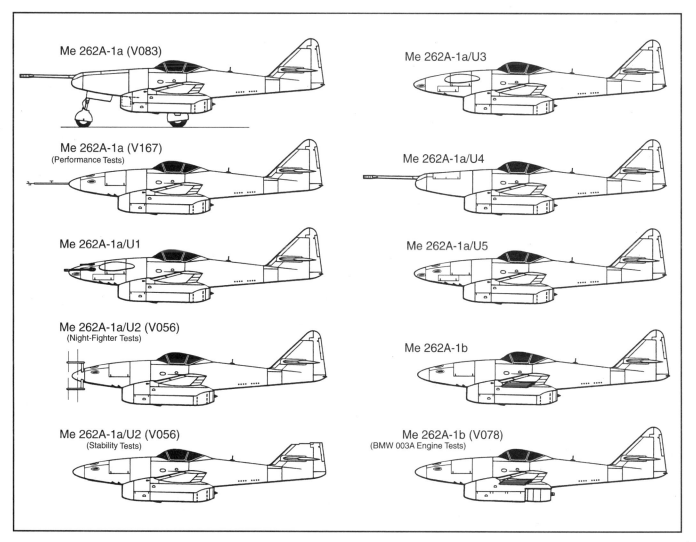

The Me 262A-1 series undoubtedly contained the most variations, simply because it was the most produced type. The differences between the original 55mm cannon prototype (V083) and the production U4 variant were subtle, just a slight change in the shape of the nose. Notice the revised nose landing gear doors on V083. V167 used an air data probe on the nose for precise measurements during performance testing. The night-fighter configuration shown for V056 is one of many tested. The second V056 drawing shows the final configuration used during stability tests, with most of the vertical stabilizer removed. Notice the difference engine nacelles on V078, used to test later variants of the BMW 003 engine. (Dennis R. Jenkins)

slots opened as soon as speed dropped to 280 MPH, and in a glide the slots opened automatically at 185 MPH. Stalling characteristics were good, and there was no tendency to fall away into a spin. There was some directional instability at large angles of yaw, but this was too marginal in impair the performance of the aircraft as a gun platform. The yaw rate was about once per cycle per second, but could be controlled relatively easily with the rudder. Various attempts were made to correct this instability, but the problem was never truly satisfactory resolved.

The Me 262A-1a flew fairly efficiently on the power on one engine at speeds of 280-310 MPH, and endurance could be extended to 2.25 hours by turning one turbojet off once an altitude of 25,000 feet had been reached. Pilots were encouraged to restart the engine prior to descending below 10,000 feet since a landing on one-engine was considered dangerous, but could be accomplished by a good pilot.

Experiments to develop a practical *air-to-air* bombing technique using the Me 262 were initiated at Rechlin in December 1944 and continued until March 1945. The standard *Revi* 16B gunsight was used during the initial tests, but in

December 1944 Dr. Kortum of Zeiss completed the development of the GPV 1 (*Gegner-Pfeil-Visier*, or Flight-Path Pointer Sight) for use by the Me 262 in air-to-air bombing. Values for the relative speeds of the Me 262 and the bomber formation to be attacked, the relative altitude from which the bombs were to be dropped, and the necessary ballistic figures for the type of bomb were fed into the GPV 1, which computed a solution to attack the formation in a 20 degree dive. It was proposed to carry out the air-to-air bombing attacks with a formation of four Me 262s, and the bombers were to be approached from ahead and about 3,000 feet above. Six single-seat Me 262s were fitted with the GPV 1 gunsight in January 1945 and used either one AB 500 (1,102-pound) or two SC 250 (551-pound) bombs to attack American bomber formations. Records from *Kommando Stamp*, the only unit to fly this type of mission, indicate that some success was attained with the AB 500 bombs, but no confirmed kills were recorded with the smaller weapons.

The later variants of the Juno 004B-series more than doubled the operational life of the engine from ten to 25 hours. Compare this to 1996 when it is not uncommon for a large turbofan to remain 'on the wing' of an airliner for more than 20,000 hours. The engines were also slightly more forgiving, and allowed more abrupt throttle handling without bursting into flames, a trait that had not endeared the earlier engines to the pilots. And by January 1945 the geared control column first tested on the Me 262V10 was finally being installed in some operational aircraft. These changes made the Me 262 a much easier aircraft to fly, especially for inexperienced pilots.

By 10 January 1945 over 600 Me 262s had been accepted by the *Luftwaffe*. Interestingly, after their acceptance flights, most early aircraft were partially disassembled and shipped by rail to their units. Since the Allies were concentrating on disrupting German rail service, a fairly large number of these aircraft were not reaching their destinations and the *Luftwaffe* Quartermaster-General listed only 61 aircraft as being in service with operational squadrons:

The second Me 262A-2a/U2 (Werk-Nr. 110555) was slightly different than the first, sprouting two pitot booms ahead of the bombardier's position. The bombardier lay prone in the glazed nose, sighting through a Lotfe *7H bombsight. (Air Force Museum Collection)*

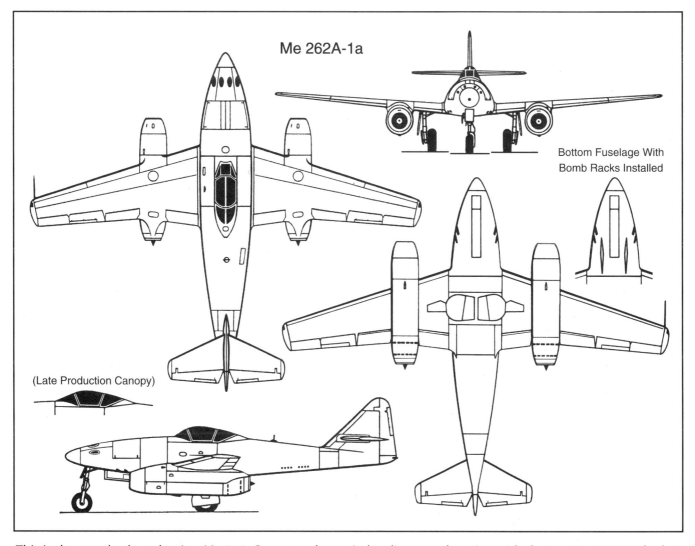

Me 262A-1a

Bottom Fuselage With
Bomb Racks Installed

(Late Production Canopy)

This is the standard production Me 262. Compare the main landing gear location with that on Me 262V1. The late production canopy apparently was used on very few aircraft. Generally a wire antenna (not illustrated) was strung between the rear of the cockpit canopy and the top of the vertical stabilizer. (Dennis R. Jenkins)

I.Gruppe of *Kampfgeschwader (KG) 51*; fighter-bombers; 27

II.Gruppe of *Kampfgeschwader (KG) 51*; fighter-bombers; 25

10.Gruppe of *Nachtjagdgeschwader (NJG) 11* (ex-*EKdo Welter*); night-fighters; 4

Nahaufklärungsgruppe (NAGr) 6 (ex-*Kdo Braunegg)*; reconnaissance; 5

Probably three times as many were in service with new groups that were in the process of forming up, and a further 150 had been destroyed by Allied action or in accidents. It is interesting to note that the Quartermaster-General listed no Me 262 day fighters in operational service, even though this was two months after Hitler had released the aircraft for this mission.

Most of the new units were operational within a couple of months, and on 3 March 1945, the Me 262 fighter units made their first determined efforts to engage Allied bomber formations. Twenty-nine fighters were launched against American raids on Magdeburg, Brunswick, Hannover, and Chemnitz with conflicting results. The Germans claimed six bombers and two fighters destroyed at a cost of a single Me 262. The Americans listed three bombers and six fighters lost with no mention of an Me 262 downed.

At least one aircraft was modified to carry a pair of 210mm *Wurfgranate* (Wgr) 21 spin-stabilized air-to-air rockets in tubes installed on the *Wikinger-Schiff* (Viking Ship) weapons pylons below the forward fuselage. This was an adaptation of the *Nebelwerfer* multiple-barrel

A single Me 262A-1a (Werk-Nr. 130083, V083) was converted to carry a Rheinmetall 50MM BK 5 cannon. This necessitated modifying the nose landing gear considerably (compare the landing gear doors with normal Me 262s). The construction of the Me 262 encouraged one-off designs since the entire nose section was built as a separate unit and was bolted on. (Jay Miller Collection via the Aerospace Education Center)

rocket launcher used by the ground forces. However, the Wgr 21 proved to be too slow for accurate aiming, and was not placed into operational service.

A far more satisfactory solution to the problem was provided by the R4M air-to-air rocket designed by Kurt Heber and manufactured by Deutsche Waffen-und Muni-

tionsfabrik at Lübeck. The 55MM R4M (*Rakete—4 kg—Minengeschoss,* literally, rocket—8.8 pound—thin-walled shell) contained 17.6 ounces of Hexogen

Two examples of the Me 262A-1a/U4 (Werk-Nr. 111899 and 170083) were constructed. A Rheinmetall-Mauser 50MM MK 214A cannon was fitted instead of the BK 5 used on V083. The second example (pictured) was captured by the Americans, but an attempt to bring it back to the United States failed when the aircraft crashed on a ferry flight. (Air Force Museum Collection)

Another victim of the Me 262's weak nose gear. This is an Me 262A-1a/U3 interim reconnaissance variant. Noteworthy is the covered over 30MM gun port on the fuselage side and the relocated 30MM gun in the extreme nose. The film magazines for the two RB 20/30 cameras are clearly visible, as is the 'bulge' necessary to provide clearance for them. (Air Force Museum Collection)

explosive and could cause considerable damage. The trajectory of the R4M was almost the same as the that of the MK 108 cannon, and therefore enabled the standard *Revi* 16B gunsight to be used. A simple wooden launching rack was designed to carry 12 rockets, one rack being mounted under each wing as standard armament on the Me 262A-1b. The entire battery of 24 rockets were launched within a

The Me 262A-1a/U4 (Werk-Nr. 111899) retained the gun camera in the normal position in the extreme nose. The V083 prototype's cannon installation had deleted the gun camera, and is one way to differentiate between the prototype and the final configuration. (Air Force Museum Collection)

Wilma Jeanne was the second Me 262A-1a/U4 (Werk-Nr. 170083). When Colonel Watson took possession of the aircraft, the name was changed to Happy Hunter II. *The aircraft crashed after taking off from Melun France on 11 June 1945 while being ferried to Cherbourg to be sent to the United States.* (Air Force Museum Collection)

FE-111 was an Me 262A-1a/U3 interim reconnaissance version captured by the Americans. This aircraft was initially named 'Dennis' and is now in the National Air and Space Museum. The bulge required to cover the camera installation is clearly visible. This particular aircraft does not appear to have been fitted with the single 30MM cannon installed on some. (Air Force Museum Collection)

space of 0.03 second, and scattered to cover an area that would be occupied by a four-engined bomber at a distance of 1,800 feet. Tests were conducted with one Me 262A-1b fitted with 17 R4M rockets beneath each wing, and it was planned to mount as many as 24 per wing for even greater effect.

On 18 March 1945, a total of 37 jet fighters were launched against 1,221 bombers escorted by 632 fighters that were attacking Berlin. During this attack the R4M air-to-air rocket was used by the Me 262 for the first time, with devastating results. Twelve bombers and two fighters were claimed by the Germans (the Americans acknowledge only eight of the bombers), with a loss of two Me 262s.

A more sophisticated rocket designed by Dr. Max Kramer was the Ruhrstahl X4 which weighed 132 pounds and was 5.95 feet long. The rocket was guided by impulses transmitted from the launch aircraft by

means of two wires. The X4 would be launched at a range of 1,000 feet and was equipped with both impact and acoustic fuses. Four X4 rockets were to have been mounted beneath the wings of the Me 262, and some stability tests were conducted with *Werk-Nr.* 111944 equipped with mock-ups of the rocket. No 'live' tests had been conducted prior to the end of the war, primarily because the factory that produced the rocket's BMW 109-548 liquid-fueled engine was destroyed by Allied bombers before sufficient quantities had been produced.

Other weapons intended for the Me 262 in its bomber interceptor role included the 242-pound R100/BS rocket, which used a warhead consisting of 400 incendiary pellets. Some aerodynamic trials were undertaken by *Werk-Nr.* 111944 with an R100/BS mounted on each bomb pylon beneath the fuselage, but none were ever launched.

Various alternative or supplementary

Lady Jess IV was an Me 262A-1a/U3 interim reconnaissance variant. It was sent back to the United Sates where it was assigned Navy BuNo 121443. It crashed on 7 November 1945 at NAS Patuxtant River, and was subsequently scrapped.

The Army Air Force shows off its captured German aircraft in October 1945 at Wright Field. Me 262A-1a (Werk-Nr. 500491) is in the foreground, with an Me 163 and Fw 190 behind it. Although hard to discern, the Swallow has a red nose cap, fin cap, and windshield frame. This aircraft is now in the NASM. (Air Force Museum Collection)

conventional weapons were also considered for the *Schwalbe* since the standard quartet of 30MM MK 108 cannon was not entirely satisfactory. This weapon still tended to jam when the fighter maneuvered, a fact which did not please its pilots. The **Me 262A-1a/U1** featured a nose-mounted armament of two 20MM MG 151 cannon with 146 rounds each, two 30MM MK 108 cannon with 66 rounds each, and two 30MM MK 103 cannon with 72 rounds each. Compared with the MK 108, the MK 103 had a longer barrel, a muzzle brake, and a higher muzzle velocity. The size of the MK 103 and its ammunition feed system necessitated the introduction of a bulged fairing on each side of the fuselage nose. This combination of three different cannon was not adopted as a production configuration, and only three examples of the Me 262A-1a/U1 were built.

A more potent weapon was provided by the Rheinmetall 50MM BK 5 cannon installed in an Me 262A-1a (*Werk-Nr.* 130083). Bruno Nitza-

(Left and opposite page) Me 262A-1a/U3 (Werk-Nr. Unknown) was surrendered to US forces at Lechfeld. After it arrived in the US, it was used to compare performance with a Lockheed P-80. As part of these tests, the aircraft was extensively reconditioned and a great deal of attention was paid to giving the exterior a smooth finish to minimize drag. During this process, the normal 'bulged' reconnaissance nose was removed and replaced with a fighter nose. The aircraft is now in the Planes of Fame Museum in Chino, California, wearing incorrect markings identifying it as Werk-Nr. 111617, which was scrapped near Munich in 1945. (Air Force Museum Collection)

cke was in charge of the project, which began in January 1945 and had an aircraft flying in the brief period of four weeks. The BK 5 was installed well forward of the center of gravity, necessitating the installation of ballast in the rear fuselage, all of which limited the aircraft to 525 MPH. Somewhat surprisingly, the installation, including the barrel that projected almost seven feet ahead of the fuselage, had no adverse affects on the Me 262's handling, although the aircraft did have a pronounced yaw every time the weapon was fired. The nose wheel also had to be modified so that it swiveled to lie flat beneath the weapon, along with changes to the nose-wheel doors. The BK 5 installation eliminated the gun camera normally mounted in the extreme nose of the Me 262, something that would have to be corrected if the weapon was to enter production. Two other Me 262A-1a fighters were fitted with the BK 5, but were restricted to ground firing trials.

The Me 262's most successful day was probably 31 March 1945. A total of 38 sorties against American and British bombers resulted in the loss of 14 bombers and two fighters, with no recorded Me 262 losses. By the end of the first week of April, more than 1,200 Me 262s had been accepted by the *Luftwaffe*, but fewer than 200 aircraft were assigned to operational units as follows:

Stab/Jagdeschwader (JG) 7; fighters; 5

I.Gruppe of *Jagdeschwader (JG) 7*; fighters; 41

III.Gruppe of *Jagdeschwader (JG) 7*; fighters; 30

Jagdverband (JV) 44; fighters; ~50

I.Gruppe of *Kampfgeschwader (KG)(J) 54;* fighters; 37

10.Gruppe of *Nachtjagdgeschwader (NJG) 11;* night-fighters; ~9

I.Gruppe of *Kampfgeschwader (KG) 51;* fighter-bombers; 15

II.Gruppe of *Kampfgeschwader (KG) 51;* fighter-bombers; 6

Nahaufklärungsgruppe (NAGr) 6; reconnaissance; 7

The figure of 200 operational Me 262s would never be exceeded by the *Luftwaffe.* Of the thousand others that had been built, over half had been destroyed by the Allies, many without ever having flown an operational sortie. Another hundred served with units either training to enter combat, or withdrawn from combat for rest. The remain-der sat, unused, on railway sidings or airfields.

The 55 sorties conducted by Me 262s on 10 April 1945 would mark the greatest number of missions flown in a single day. The Germans managed to destroy 10 American bombers, however, 27 jet fighters, almost half the number which had taken off, were destroyed. By the end of the war, USAAF fighters had shot down almost 100 Me 262s, with the RAF accounting for another 30, and the heavy bombers themselves claiming ten.

The lone **Me 262A-1a/U2** (*Werk-Nr.* 170056, V056) had a FuG 220 Lichtenstein SN 2 radar and *Hirschgeweih* antenna array installed in the nose to test night-fighter concepts. Karl Baur flew V056 equipped with various nose-mounted antenna arrays and verti-cal blade antennas mounted on the wings to provide information about the behavior of the antennas at high speed, and help engineers determine the most favorable shape and location for the antennas themselves. In addition, the flights were to ensure that the antennas would be able to remain fully functional when the four MK 108 cannon were fired. The aircraft was later assigned to *Kommando Welter* and used with some success until the delivery of true Me 262B-1a/U1 night-fighters. During February 1945 the FuG 220 was replaced by an experimental FuG 226 *Neul-ing* radar, but the aircraft was heavi-ly damaged during a landing acci-dent shortly thereafter, and no seri-ous testing was conducted.

During the spring of 1945, yet another unit was formed: the *Ein-satzkommando Braunegg,* a photo-reconnaissance unit equipped with Bf 109Gs and **Me 262A-1a/U3**s. These were fighter models modi-fied by the removal of armament

The Air Force Museum's Me 262A-1a wore a very basic paint scheme while it sat outside during the late 1950s and early 1960s. The aircraft was in basically good repair, although it did suffer some corrosion damage, particularly to the steel nose section. Unfortunately, the Werk-Nr. of this aircraft is unknown. (Air Force Museum Collection)

This is the Air Force Museum's Me 262A-1a while undergoing tests at NAS Patuxtant River on 2 August 1946. The Navy assigned the aircraft Bureau Number (BuNo) 121442, while Watson's Whizzers had given the aircraft the name Screemin' Meemie. The aircraft flew tests for the Navy until 31 January 1947. It was eventually salvaged from the aircraft dump at Pax River in 1957 and transferred to the Museum.

An Me 262A-1a emerges from the final assembly line at one of the 'forest factories'. From here the aircraft would be towed a short distance away to perform gun firing and engine run up tests, then to an Autobahn for its delivery flight. (Air Force Museum Collection)

Another Me 262A-1a damaged from Allied bomb attacks. The port engine has been removed, perhaps to install on a more serviceable aircraft. (Air Force Museum Collection)

A production Me 262A-1a before delivery to the Luftwaffe. The letters on the fuselage side are not unit identification markings, but the radio call sign allocated for factory test flights. (Air Force Museum Collection)

and the installation of either two RB 20/30 cameras, or one RB 20/30 and one RB 75/30 cameras mounted beside the nose gear wheel well. A glass window was fitted in the cockpit floor to allow the pilot to see what he photographed. A few aircraft managed to retain a single 30MM MK 108 cannon along with the camera equipment. A bulge, similar to the ones used on the Me 262A-1a/U1 was fitted to each side of the fuselage to cover the camera's film magazine.

A design study was performed for the installation of a 55MM MK 114 cannon in a nose similar to that used to mount the 50MM BK 5 cannon. Plans to mount this weapon were abandoned in favor of the Rheinmetall-Mauser 50MM MK 214A high-velocity cannon which was installed in two Me 262A-1a (*Werk-Nrs.* 111899 and 170083) that were redesignated **Me 262A-1a/U4** *Pulkzerstörer*. This was a modified version of a cannon original designed to be mounted in light tanks, and fired a shell weighing 3.3 pounds over an effective range of 3,300 feet. Mounted in a slightly recontoured nose in place of the original four 30MM cannon, the cannon's rate of fire was 150 rounds per minute, and a single hit was probably sufficient to destroy even a heavy bomber. Unlike the original BK 5 prototype, this installation retained the normal nose gun camera. The recoil system installed was so effective that almost none was transmitted to the airframe, and post-war testing showed the pilot

This Me 262A-2a is sitting beside an Autobahn near Leipheim in 1945. This particular forest factory painted the aircraft in a basic camouflage scheme prior to delivery. (Air Force Museum Collection)

An Me 262A-1a from Erprobungskommando *262. The large '4', as well as a band around the fuselage just aft of the cockpit, were painted in yellow. The port engine had been replaced a few days earlier when it ingested mud from the airfield during a take-off attempt. Since the front cowling was usually replaced with the engine, this explains the difference on color. (Air Force Museum Collection)*

Me 262A-1a *(Werk-Nr. 500491) at Lager Lechfeld after its capture. Originally this was* Yellow 7 *of IV./JG 7. It was later given the Whizzers' number 888 and the name* Ginny H. *(Jay Miller Collection via the Aerospace Education Center)*

and components for a further 60 were found by US ground forces at Oetztal.

Only a single **Me 262A-1a/U5** (*Werk-Nr.* 111355) was built to test an installation of six 30MM MK 108 cannon with 80 rounds per gun. However no solution was ever found to the feed system jamming problems that seemed to plague all MK 108 installations.

was barely aware of the cannon's firing.

Messerschmitt pilots Hofmann, Baur, and Lindner, and *Luftwaffe Major* Herget flew the *Pulkzerstörer* (formation destroyer) during the course of its testing at Lager-Lech-feld in March and April 1945. The second Me 262A-1a/U4 (*Werk-Nr.* 170083) was captured by the Americans, but crashed near Cherbourg on 18 July 1945 while on a ferry flight prior to being shipped to the United States. The Germans had completed ten MK 214A cannon,

Beginning in January 1945, about 150 **Me 262A-1b** fighters received a new Askania-Werke EZ 42 computing gun-sight, which was the *Luftwaffe* equivalent of the American K-14 computing gunsight fitted to the P-51D. Unfortunately, it did not function nearly as well, and in fact, the sight graticule was normally fixed in position so that it functioned the

A standard production Me 262A-1a shows the swept leading edges on both the wing and horizontal stabilizer. This aircraft wears a solid color camouflage, indicating it was probably produced by one of the forest factories late in the war. (Jay Miller Collection via the Aerospace Education Center)

This Me 262A-2a has empty bomb pylons under the forward fuselage, and only the lower two 30мм cannon installed. Although not mentioned in Messerschmitt documentation, many operational Me 262A-2a aircraft had their upper two cannon removed, perhaps in an attempt to better balance the aircraft. The upper gun ports were then covered by doped fabric. (Air Force Museum Collection)

The Lichtenstein SN 2 radar was installed on Me 262A-1a/U2 (Werk-Nr. 170056, V056) as a testbed for the night-fighter concept. V056 flew with several antenna configurations in an attempt to find one that imposed the smallest performance penalty. The radar antenna array shown here is not the same configuration used on production Me 262B-1a/U1 night-fighters. Here each antenna is angled about 25 degrees from the production units, and are slightly different in shape. (Air Force Museum Collection)

WARBIRD**TECH**
SERIES

The Me 262A-1a at The Planes of Fame Museum at Chino, California after its 1968 restoration. Unfortunately, available records do not indicate what the original Werknummern *of this aircraft is. It has been reported that this aircraft and the Me 262 at the Air Force Museum exchanged noses shortly after arriving in the United States.* (Jay Miller Collection via the Aerospace Education Center)

same way as the old *Revi* 16B. These Me 262A-1b fighters also had provisions for carrying 24 R4M air-to-air rockets under the wings, but otherwise differed little from the Me 262A-1a configuration.

It should be noted that some sources (and many books) list the production Me 262A-1b (as described above) as either a standard Me 262A-1a or as the **Me 262A-1a/R1**, and assign the Me 262A-1b designation to a never-built BMW 003A powered production aircraft similar to V078 (described below). It is believed that this is incorrect, and the proper designations are presented here.

A lone Me 262A-1b (*Werk-Nr.* 170078), also known as Me 262V078, was flown by Karl Baur and Gerd Lindner during December 1944 in an attempt to flight

qualify the BMW 003A-1 engine. The results showed that this powerplant was still inferior to the Jumo 004 used in production aircraft, but that it nevertheless held great promise. In fact, the short flight test program went through four different BMW engines, all being replaced due to various failures. Production aircraft would continue to use the Jumo engine, although development of the BMW engine continued.

The fighter-bomber version of the Me 262, which received the appellation *Sturmvogel* (Stormbird) to distinguish it from those aircraft completed purely as fighters, began to leave the assembly lines in July 1944. The initial sub-type, the **Me 262A-2a**, differed from the Me 262A-1a solely in having bomb-fusing equipment and a pair of pylons from which two 551-pound

bombs or a single 1,102-pound bomb could be hung. The under-fuselage pylons could carry either *Wikinger-Schiff*, ETC 504, or Schloss 503 bomb racks. An additional fuselage fuel tank was installed behind the cockpit, and the aircraft's maximum take-off weight increased by approximately 700 pounds. Bombing attacks were intended to be made in a 30 degree dive at a speed for 530-560 MPH with the pilot leveling off at 3,000-3,500 feet just prior to bomb release.

Two aircraft (*Werk-Nrs.* 130170 and 138188) were fitted with a Zeiss TSA (*Tief-und-Sturz-fluganlage*—Low-and-Diving- flight device) in the extreme nose and delivered to Rechlin for trials under the designation **Me 262A-2a/U1**. These aircraft had the two lower MK 108 cannon removed to make room for the TSA devices. Two further aircraft (*Werk-Nrs*. 130164 and 170070) were fitted with improved TSA 2A systems, but before any conclusive results could be ascertained, Hitler released the Me 262 as a fighter and interest in the bomber versions rapidly faded.

Although the externally-mounted bombs reduced the speed of the Me 262A-2a en-route to its target to the extent that it could be intercepted by conventional fighters, the high speeds attained by the *Sturmvogel* during its diving attack itself enabled it to fulfill its mission in conditions of complete Allied air superiority. Bombing results were as accurate as those achieved by

the Fw 190, but one disadvantage of the Me 262A-2a was that its high speed rendered identification of small targets virtually impossible. The usual practice was to approach the target in level flight until it disappeared from sight under the port or starboard engine, and then commence the diving attack. It was essential to empty the rear main tank before pulling out of the dive as the aircraft was otherwise tail heavy and tended to nose up suddenly when the bombs were released.

In an attempt to improve bombing accuracy, one aircraft (*Werk-Nr.* 110484) was modified in October

1944 to permit the installation of a gyro-stabilized *Lotfe* 7H bomb sight and designated **Me 262A-2a/U2**. This bomb sight necessitated the accommodation of a second crew member, and therefore all cannon armament was removed and a new wood and plexiglass nose section was installed that allowed the bombardier to lay prone and sight the target with the *Lotfe* 7H sight. Potential bomb loads were identical to those carried by the standard Me 262A-2a. In early January 1945, V484 was joined by the similarly equipped V555 (*Werk-Nr.* 110555) and soon afterwards, both aircraft were equipped with Siemens K 22 autopilots. Tests by Karl Baur and

A single-seat Avia S-92 in the VM Aviation and Space Flight Museum in Kbeli. This aircraft was assembled from an uncompleted Me 262A-1a and used Jumo 004B-2 engines. There were initial plans to modify the aircraft with stronger landing gear and BMW 003 engines, but these were overcome by the availability of inexpensive Soviet MiG fighters. (Jay Miller Collection via the Aerospace Education Center)

Gerd Lindner indicated the system was probably satisfactory for its intended role as a high-speed bomber, but that the Ar 234 fulfilled this role better.

Some attempt was made to employ the Me 262 for ground strafing missions, but the aircraft was poorly suited for this role. The MK 108 cannon had so low a muzzle velocity that the attack had to be made from an altitude below 1,500 feet to achieve any accuracy, and the 360 rounds of ammunition carried were inadequate for the amount of target area that could be covered by the fast moving jet. Furthermore, the limited armor fitted was inadequate to protect the aircraft from ground fire. This resulted in the appearance of the **Me 262A-3a** intended specifically for the ground support role. Although the standard cannon armament and ammunition capacity were retained, armor protection was added for

Two SC 250 (551-pound) bombs mounted on an Me 262A-2a. One of the bombs has a complete set of boxed fins, the other does not have the box. This was the typical bomb load for the Me 262, although two 1,002-pound or a single 2,205-pound bomb could be carried instead. (Air Force Museum Collection)

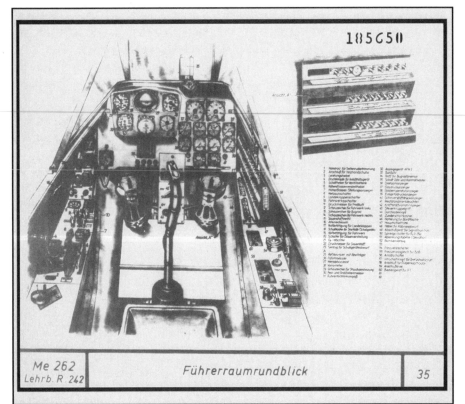

This is the illustration used in the original Me 262A-2a pilot's handbook. Compared to USAAF and RAF documents, this was an extremely sketchy handbook from which one was expected to learn about the most complex fighter of its era. But an experienced cadre within each squadron assisted newcomers, and the Me 262's pilot error rate was not particularly higher than its contemporaries. (Air Force Museum Collection)

the fuel tanks, as well as the floor and sidewalls of the cockpit. The series did not enter production, and not even a prototype was completed.

Reconnaissance variants had been discussed as early as 26 September 1941, and a forward fuselage cockpit mockup of a camera-equipped model had been inspected by the RLM on 5 February 1942. One of the original pre-production aircraft was to have been modified as a reconnaissance prototype, but this was overcome by other events. Some reports indicate that an unarmed tactical reconnaissance aircraft was to receive the **Me 262A-4a** designation, but no conclusive documentation has been uncovered to confirm this.

The **Me 262A-5a** reconnaissance fighter, initially proposed on 21 February 1945, was a refinement of the interim Me 262A-1a/U3. The aircraft had two side-by-side obliquely-mounted cameras, either two RB 50/30s or an RB 20/30 and an RB 75/30. A small observation window was incorporated into the floor of the cockpit, and cannon armament was reduced to two MK 108s with 65 rounds per gun. The Me 262A-5a retained the bomb pylons of the *Sturmvogel* which were employed to carry two 79 gallon fuel tanks or a single 159 gallon tank. A single prototype was under construction at the end of the war.

The bomb arming and fusing panel on Me 262A-2a aircraft was located below the main instrument panel between the pilot's legs. The instrumentation installed in various Me 262 aircraft differed considerably, one assumes based on what was available at the time of manufacture. (Air Force Museum Collection)

THE ME 262 IN COLOR

It is hard to realize that color photography was still somewhat rare during World War Two. It was even rarer in Germany late during the war. Resources were scarce, and color film was hard to come by.

What film existed was of fairly poor quality, and many of the images have become unusable as the years have passed. Therefore, there is relatively little color photography of operational Me 262s.

Most of the color photograph that exists on the Me 262 is of one of the museum birds, although the Tischler aircraft will soon present an entire generation with new opportunities to photograph the first operational jet fighter.

In order to present some new images, this color section used the Air Force Museum's original Me 262 as a subject, as well as in-process shots of the Tischler aircraft from the summer of 1996.

Since many Me 262s were not painted when they left the forest factories, that task being left to the first unit they served with, it is difficult to determine the authenticity of any given paint scheme. The camouflage on this Me 262A1 was not the most prevalent, but was frequently seen on aircraft from certain squadrons. (Air Force Museum Collection)

The first three Tischler airplanes in various states of assembly. The use of plywood in the nose section is authentic. (Dennis R. Jenkins)

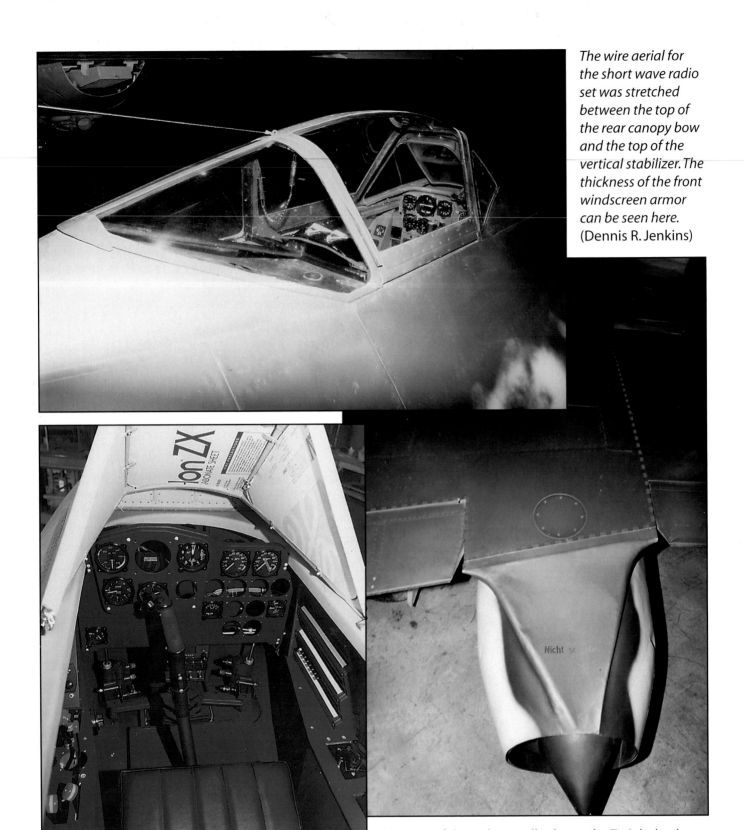

The wire aerial for the short wave radio set was stretched between the top of the rear canopy bow and the top of the vertical stabilizer. The thickness of the front windscreen armor can be seen here. (Dennis R. Jenkins)

The cockpit of the first Tischler aircraft after it has been installed. The only concession to modern technology (besides the engines) is a small avionics stack on the bottom-center of the main instrument panel where the bomb fusing panel should be. (Jay Miller)

The rear of the right nacelle shows the Zwiebel exhaust cone. Initially this cone was manually adjusted by the pilot, but later models (such as the Air Force Museum's, shown here) had automatically adjusting units. This was accomplished by using ram air coming through the nacelle to push against a spring-loaded plate. (Dennis R. Jenkins)

The ejector chutes for the 30MM MK 108 cannon on the #1 Tischler airplane. A second set of these chutes is on the other side of the fuselage. The narrow opening behind the ejector chutes is the nose wheel well, while the larger opening to the right is the access to the forward fuel tanks. (Dennis R. Jenkins)

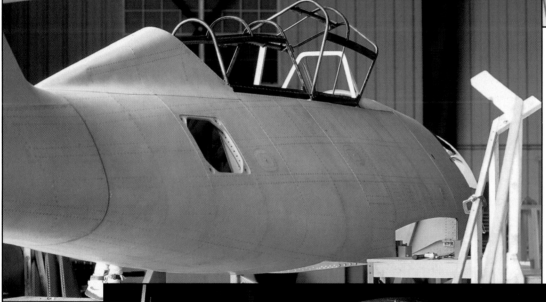

The fuselage of the #1 Tischler airplane takes shape at the Texas Airplane Factory. The large removable panel allows access to the push-pull control rods, compass and radio equipment in the aft-fuselage. (Dennis R. Jenkins)

The right engine nacelle of the Air Force Museum's aircraft. The starter motor for the Jumo 004B was housed in the bullet immediately inside the nacelle. (Dennis R. Jenkins)

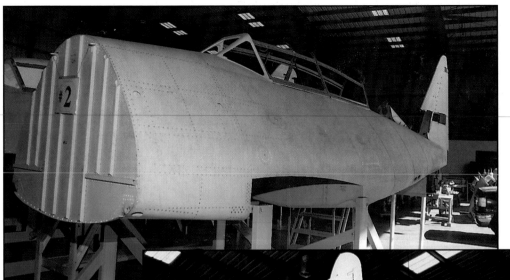

The mid and aft-fuselage of the #2 Tischler aircraft. This is a two-seater, and it already has most of the canopy frame installed. The bolt holes to attach the nose section are visible at the bottom corners of the triangular fuselage, and the two brackets for the top torque-tubes are being used to hang the '#2' sign. (Jay Miller)

The #3, #4, and #5 Tischler aircraft. Although the rudder and vertical stabilizer have been fitted to the #5 aircraft here, they will have to be removed since the horizontal stabilizer is not yet installed. Most likely they were in place for a fit-check only. (Dennis R. Jenkins)

A real Jumo 004B sits in a jig at the Texas Airplane Factory. This engine was used to create forms to cast perfect replicas that will house the General Electric J-85 engines used by Tischler's aircraft. (Jay Miller)

NOCTURNAL 6 SWALLOWS

Pilot training, or the lack of it, was rapidly becoming an issue with the Me 262. While the Me 262 was not a particularly difficult aircraft to fly in so far as experienced pilots were concerned, like all aircraft it had its share of idiosyncrasies, and some problems arose in the conversion of inexperienced pilots who had just completed their fighter training on piston-engine types. *Erprobungskommando 262* was ini-

tially responsible for conversion training at Lager-Lechfeld. Attrition was heavy, although amazingly, less than one-fifth of all training accidents in the Me 262 were directly attributable to pilot error. Approximately two-thirds were equally divided between landing gear and engine failures, with the remainder being attributed to various causes including structural failures. Nevertheless, it was obvious that training could be enhanced by providing a

dual-control two-seat variant. Accordingly, Messerschmitt evolved the **Me 262B-1a** conversion trainer converted from single-seat Me 262A-1a fighters by Blöhm und Voss.

The Me 262B-1a differed from the standard single-seater by providing a second seat for the instructor in place of the normal aft fuel tanks. Smaller, 105 gallon and 68 gallon fuel tanks were fitted behind the

Me 262B-1a/U1 (Werk-Nr. 110306) on display in Washington D.C. on 1 August 1946. At this point the aircraft was still flyable although the Hirschgeweih *radar array had been removed from the nose, and most probably the radar equipment itself. This is the same aircraft as FE-610, the designation simply changing to T2-610. The last reported location of the aircraft was at Cornell University in the early 1950s. (Air Force Museum Collection)*

second seat, and provisions were fitted to carry of two 79 gallon auxiliary tanks on the *Wikinger-Schiff* pylons beneath the forward fuselage. Full dual controls were provided, and standard cannon armament was retained, but only 15 examples of this trainer were delivered.

In early September 1944 an effort was initiated to develop the **Me 262B-1a/U1** radar-equipped nightfighter based on the two-seat Me 262B-1a trainer. The decision to use the Me 262 in the night fighting role stemmed from a series of trials performed at Rechlin in October

1944 with the Me 262A-1a/U2 (V056) fitted with a Lichtenstein SN-2 (FuG 220) intercept radar with a four-pole *Hirschgeweih* antenna array. Messerschmitt continued to build single seat fighters, which were then shipped to Blöhm und Voss to be converted into two-

In 1946 Me 262B-1a/U1 (Werk-Nr. 110306) was in the same basic configuration it was captured in. The Hirschgeweih *radar array is still mounted on the nose, and two drop tanks are carried beneath the fuselage. The FE-610 number has replaced the Whizzers' number 999 and* Ole Fruit Cake *name. (Air Force Museum Collection)*

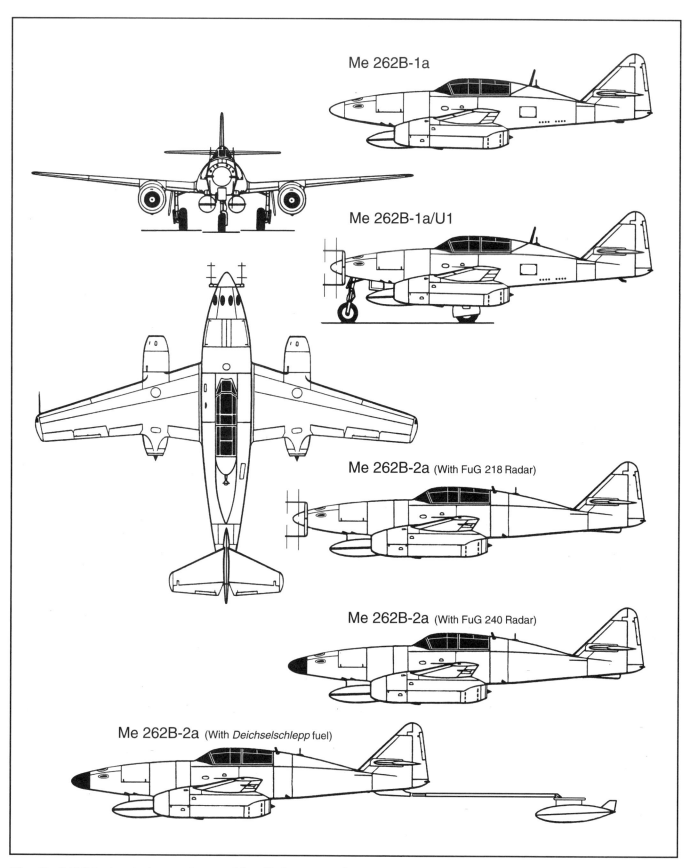

Me 262B-1a

Me 262B-1a/U1

Me 262B-2a (With FuG 218 Radar)

Me 262B-2a (With FuG 240 Radar)

Me 262B-2a (With *Deichselschlepp* fuel)

The Me 262B is the easiest variant to identify because of its extended canopy and two seats. The B-2a featured a stretched fuselage, with 'plug' sections inserted immediately forward and aft of the cockpit. Noteworthy are the 30mm cannon aimed upward on the B-2a variants. (Dennis R. Jenkins)

Me 262B-1a/U1 (Werk-Nr. 110306) FE-610 became T2-610 although the Whizzers' logo is still on the nose. The Hirschgeweih *radar array was removed from the nose to improve the speed and handling of the aircraft during flight tests.* (Erwin Bulban from the Jay Miller Collection via the Aerospace Education Center)

A night-fighter Me 262B-1a/U1 (Werk-Nr. 110306) was surrendered to British forces at Schleswig in May 1945, and allocated to the USAAF as 'USA2.' Subsequently it was allocated Whizzer's number 999 and the name Ole Fruit Cake. *It became FE-610 upon arrival at Freeman Field in September 1945 and was later reassigned as T2-610.* (Erwin Bulban from the Jay Miller Collection via the Aerospace Education Center)

The Heimatschützer I *prototype Me 262C-1a (Werk-Nr. 130186) used a Walter R II-211/3 (HWK 509A-1) rocket engine mounted in the aft fuselage to achieve a substantial increase in rate-of-climb. The rocket provided 3,750 lbf thrust for three minutes, enabling the aircraft to reach 26,250 feet in 4.5 minutes.* (Jay Miller Collection via the Aerospace Education Center)

seaters, then to the main workshops of Deutsche Lufthansa at Berlin-Staaken for conversion to night-fighters. The latter work primarily involved the installation of FuG 218 *Neptun V* radar equipment with a *Hirschgeweih* array and a slight alteration of the fuel feed system. The display and control units for the radar were located in the rear cockpit in place of the trainer's second set of controls. The drag of the *Hirschgeweih* array, with its eight 7mm-diameter dipoles, was such that it reduced the maximum speed of the aircraft by 37 MPH, but it was still faster than all Allied fighters. Messerschmitt saw this model as strictly an interim model pending the development of the Me 262B-2a dedicated night-fighter. *Kommando Welter* was destined to be the only *Luftwaffe* night fighter unit to equip with the Me 262, receiving fewer than a dozen examples of the Me 262B-1a/U1 before the end of the war.

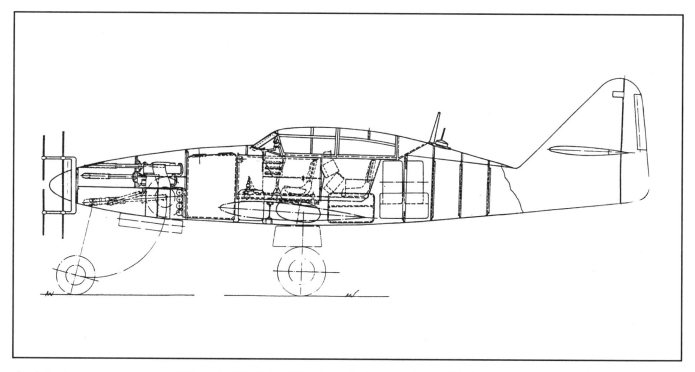

An interior arrangement of the Me 262B-1a/U1 night-fighter variant. This is from the original Messerschmitt drawings. (Dennis R. Jenkins)

Whereas the Me 262B-1a/U1 was a hurried adaptation of the training model, the **Me 262B-2a** was considered the definitive night fighting variant. The principle change consisted of the insertion of additional fuselage sections fore and aft of the tandem cockpits, increasing the overall length by 3.94 feet. This provided the necessary space to restore the 238 gallon and 159 gallon aft fuel tanks which had been replaced by 106 and 68 gallon tanks respectively in the Me 262B-1a. Simultaneously, the 44 gallon forward auxiliary tank was increased in capacity to 132 gallons, and while the two 79 gallon external drop tanks were retained, provisions was made for a 238 gallon auxiliary tank to be attached to the rear fuselage by means of a *Deichselschlepp* (pole-tow) arrangement. As with the towed bomb tested with the Me 262 earlier, the fuel tank was intended to be fitted with a wooden wing and a jettisonable two-wheel take-off dolly. The towed tank would have increased the total fuel capacity available to the Me 262B-2a to 1,163 gallons. The contents of the towed tank was to be used first, enabling the tank, its wing and tow-bar to be jettisoned at an early stage of the sortie. The Me 262B-2a retained the standard forward-firing battery of four MK 108 cannon, and in addition, provision was made for two similar weapons in a vertical *Schräge Musik* arrangement immediately aft of the rear cockpit.

The Me 262B-2a was equipped with radar similar to that of the Me 262B-1a/U1, and the first prototype commenced flight trials in March 1945. Various attempts were made to streamline the *Hirschgeweih* array, resulting in the *Morgenstern* aerial system in which shorter antennae protruded through a more pointed nose cone. It was calculated that this would restore 30 MPH but flight testing had not commenced prior to the end of the war.

The forward fuselage of an Me 262 complete with four 30MM MK 108 cannon. The cannon had very short barrels as shown here, and afforded a very compact installation. The bulkhead immediately in front of the cannon (where the barrels pass through) was made of laminated wood (plywood). (Air Force Museum Collection)

A series of 1945 US Navy photos of a captured Jumo 004B-2 turbojet engine shows the engine with all plumbing and accessories attached. Despite not having access to high-temperature materials, the Jumo engines were extremely well built, although they had very limited operating lives. (Air Force Museum Collection)

In any event, it was decided to standardize on the centimeter-wavelength FuG 240 *Berlin* radar with a dish scanner housed in a plastic radome, affording little or no drag penalty. The second example of the Me 262B-2a, which was to have flown with the *Berlin* radar, was in the final stages of assembly at the time of Germany's collapse.

The Oberammergau Project Bureau also had ambitious plans to use the latest engines and improved aerodynamics in a more capable night-fighter derived from the Me 262B-2a. However, the 12 February 1945 proposal showing a highly-modified Me 262 fuselage with severely swept (45 degree) wings and two He S011 turbojets remained strictly an academic exercise. Another proposal, this one dated 27 March 1945 showed a continuing refinement of the design, this time with slightly reduced sweep on the wings.

ME 262C SERIES—HOME PROTECTORS

In early 1945 considerable importance was attached to the rapid development of rocket-boosted *Heimatschützer* (Home Protector) versions of the Me 262 capable of climbing to intercept altitude extremely rapidly. These would at least partially make up for the lack of warning that was becoming more routine as the German early-warning radar network was destroyed by Allied attack.

The Oberammergau Project Bureau was responsible for the design and conversion of the Me 262C-series. The first of these, the **Me 262C-1a** *Heimat-schützer I*, was an Me 262A-1a (*Werk-Nr.* 130186, V186) with a 3,750 LBF Walter R II-211/3 (HWK 509A-1) bi-fuel rocket motor mounted in the rear fuselage. This was the same engine used by the Messerschmitt Me 163 *Komet* flying-wing

A burst of flame from the Jumo 004 announces it being started. During engine start and low-RPM operations the Zwiebel exhaust cone was in its retracted position. (Air Force Museum Collection)

interceptor. *T-Stoff* (hydrogen peroxide and oxyquinoline) was accommodated in the forward 238 gallon forward main tank, and *C-Stoff* (hydrazine hydrate and methanol) was in the 159 gallon rear auxiliary tank. J2 diesel fuel for the Jumo 004C turbojets was limited to the 44 gallon forward auxiliary tank and the aft 238 gallon main tank. Take-off weight for the Me 262C-1a was 17,196 pounds.

The aircraft's rudder was shortened at the bottom to accommodate the rocket exhaust, which exited at the extreme base of the aft fuselage. At the end of October 1944 the Me 262C-1a was transported overland from Oberammergau to Lager-Lechfeld. Following assembly of the aircraft, and two proving flights using the Jumo 004 turbojet engines, the first static test of the Walter rocket took place on 25 October 1944. However, it was not until 27 January 1945 that Gerd Lindner made the aircraft's first flight under rocket power.

The Walter rocket could not be ignited until the Me 262 was airborne, but once started, the R II-21⅓ motor provided full power for three minutes which was sufficient to push the Me 262C-1a to 26,250 feet in 4.5 minutes. A top speed of 629 MPH was attained during the ascent. Six more flights using rocket power would be made by V186 before Allied aircraft attacked the interceptor testbed in its blast pen on 23 March 1945 and inflicted serious damage. In the summer of 1945 the remains of the aircraft were taken to the Royal Aircraft Establishment at Farnborough England to be examined by RAF engi-

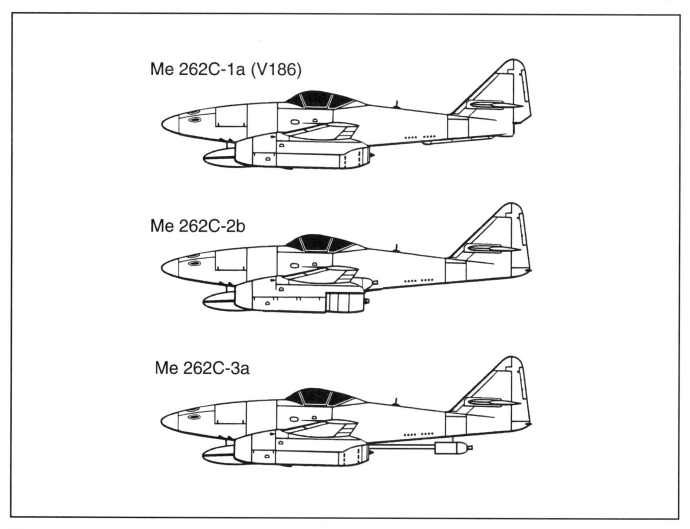

Me 262C-1a (V186)

Me 262C-2b

Me 262C-3a

The rocket assisted aircraft took decidedly different approaches. The C-1a cut off the bottom of the rudder to make room for the exhaust of a rocket carried in the rear fuselage (which was normally pretty empty). The C-2b used rocket engines integrated on top of the wing above the BMW 003 jet engines (notice the different nacelles). And the C-3a used essentially the same rocket as the C-1a, except mounted it externally so it could be jettisoned along with its external propellant tanks. (Dennis R. Jenkins)

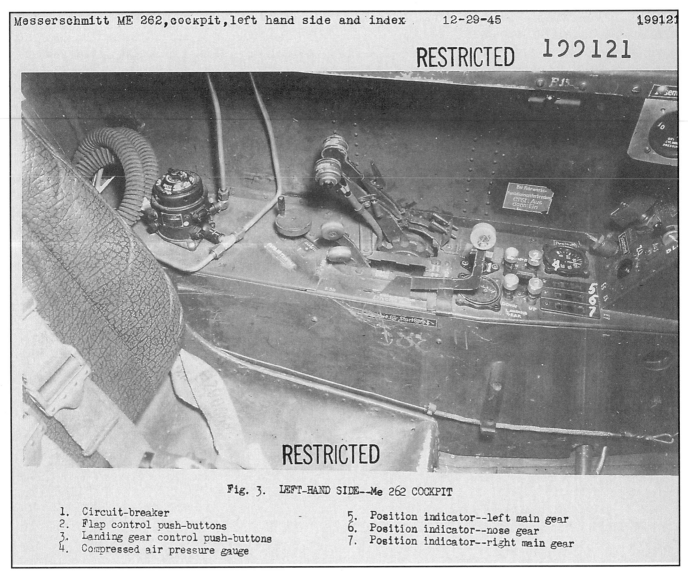

RESTRICTED   199121

RESTRICTED

Fig. 3.   LEFT-HAND SIDE--Me 262 COCKPIT

1. Circuit-breaker
2. Flap control push-buttons
3. Landing gear control push-buttons
4. Compressed air pressure gauge
5. Position indicator--left main gear
6. Position indicator--nose gear
7. Position indicator--right main gear

This photograph was used to document the Me 262 in a December 1945 report on foreign equipment. This shot illustrates the left auxiliary console that contains the throttles, and flap and landing gear switches and indicators. (Air Force Museum Collection)

neers, and the remains of the airframe were finally scrapped in 1946.

The conversion of *Werk-Nr.* 170074 (V074) into the **Me 262C-2b** was undertaken by the same group in Oberammergau, and on 20 December 1944 the *Heimatschützer II* was delivered overland to Lager-Lechfeld. The '2b' designation is somewhat illogical (it should have been Me 262C-2a), but has been explained as the 'b' representing 'BMW.'

The Me 262C-2b was powered by two BMW 003R units, each of which comprised a BMW 003A-1 turbojet of 1,760 LBF and a BMW 718 bi-fuel rocket motor rated at 2,700 LBF thrust. The arrangement of the fuel tanks was similar to that of the Me 262C-1a except that *S-Stoff* occupied the forward main tank and *R-Stoff* was housed in the aft auxiliary tank. The BMW 718 rocket motor was highly temperamental, and although 50 bench runs were made with the complete BMW 003R unit, on several occasions the rocket

engine blew up and burned fiercely.

Following reassembly of the aircraft, it too was flown on a few proving flights using jet power only. Early attempts to fly with rocket power were hampered by leaking rocket fuel, which proved highly corrosive and destroyed the sealing materials in the fuel tanks. It was not until 23 March 1945 that both TL-R engines were successfully static tested at Lager-Lechfeld.

Finally, on 26 March 1945 Karl Baur took-off under full thrust. In describing the only flight test performed with this aircraft, Karl Baur said: "I pressed the firing buttons at about 100 MPH and the rockets ignited with a roar. I had an anxious few seconds endeavoring to raise the flaps and undercarriage as the aircraft was accelerating so fast that I was momentarily afraid that they would be torn off. I held the speed back to the critical Mach number by keeping the nose high, and it seemed that I was going straight up. The fuel burned off just below 10,000 feet and I coasted on upwards to about 25,000 feet, the elapsed time from unstick being about 1.5 minutes."

The major disadvantage displayed by the first *Heimatschützer* had been the strict limitation imposed on J2 tankage by the need to use some fuel tanks for rocket propellant. The **Me 262C-3** *Heimatschützer III* therefore had a Walter R II-211/3 rocket motor slung beneath the fuselage with *C-Stoff* and *T-Stoff* carried in external tanks mounted on the bomb racks under the forward fuselage. The rocket motor was jettisonable, and was to be dropped by parachute after the propellants were consumed. Propellants were fed to the rocket motor by means of a flexible line, but difficulties were encountered with the propellant feed as the level of the tanks was slightly below that of the rocket combustion chamber, and these had not been resolved when further work on the *Heimatschützer* program was terminated.

This photograph was used to document the Me 262 in a December 1945 report on foreign equipment. This shot illustrates the left auxiliary console that contains the throttles, and flap and landing gear switches and indicators. (Air Force Museum Collection)

HIGH-SPEED Me 262s

Willy Messerschmitt had discussed fitting the Me 262 with truly swept-back wings (35 degrees) as early as April 1941 under the *Pfeilflugel I* designation. However, the priority assigned to the development and production of the initial variants had forced a temporary suspension of this work. It was not until July 1943 when testing of the Me 262 had pushed up against the effects of compressibility that the *Luftwaffe* agreed that the Me 262 could benefit from further aerodynamic refinement. In February 1944 a program was set up for 24 drop tests of a one-fifth-scale model of the Me 262 to investigate the stability behavior at high Mach numbers and the determination of the drag coefficient as a function of the Mach number. The Oberammergau Project Bureau followed this with a 'high-speed program' which discussed ways to configure a 'maximum speed aircraft.' In the course of subsequent research work, and the associated planning for new fighter and bomber aircraft, the Me 262 eventually evolved into the starting point for the program and became a testbed for the aircraft of the future.

On 1 October 1944, the Me 262V9 (*Werk-Nr*. 130004) went into the Oberammergau Project Bureau work shops for conversion to the **Me 262 HG I** (*Hochgeschwindikeit I*). The aircraft had already been involved in some high-performance testing and had received a low-profile *Rennkabine* (racing) canopy and enlarged vertical stabilizer. Oberammergau modified it further with a revised vertical stabilizer and swept-back horizontal stabilizers. There were plans to modify the inboard leading edge of the wing by enlarging the fillet significantly, but it is unclear if this ever occurred. In this form V9 began flight testing at Lager-Lechfeld on 18 January 1945. Test pilot Karl Baur complained about the low canopy and in the course of five flights discovered stability problems caused by the revised tail unit. After reverting to the older tail unit, the aircraft carried out a further 20 test flights in March 1945 with Lindner and Baur at the controls.

On 28 July 1944, Messerschmitt

This Me 262A-1a was also captured by the Americans and numbered FE-110. The inlet of the part nacelle has apparently been replaced and a Watson's Whizzers *emblem is clearly visible on the nose.* (Jay Miller Collection)

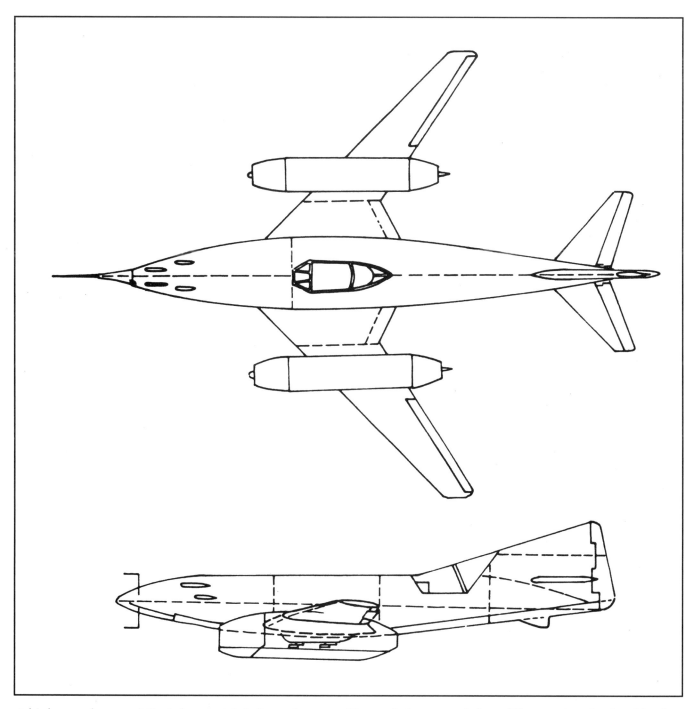

A high-speed concept that does not totally make sense. The cockpit canopy is in a different place in the side view than in the top view. Except for the basic fuselage shape, there is little resemblance to the Me 262 in this design.

proposed making significant modifications to Me 262A-1a (*Werk-Nr.* 111538). The modified aircraft was designated **Me 262 HG II**, and apart from the changes introduced on the HG I (swept horizontal surfaces and racing canopy), its main identifying feature was a wing which featured 35 degrees of sweep on the 25% MAC line. The aircraft was to be tested using both Jumo 004C and the He S011 engines. Flight tests of this configuration were intended primarily to test the wing for a future single-engine fighter that Messerschmitt was developing for the RLM. The original drawings show *Hochgeschwindikeit II* with a V-tail in place of the conventional vertical and horizontal units actually installed.

According to documents produced for the Americans in June 1945, the HG II was scheduled to begin flight tests in mid-March 1945. However, the aircraft was

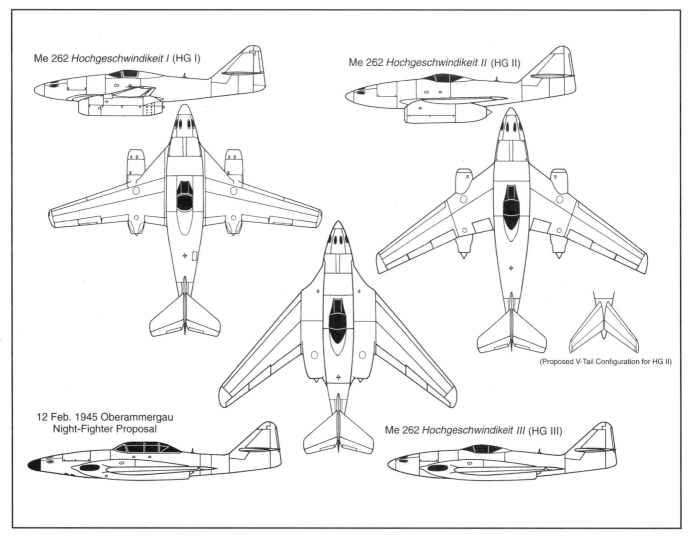

Me 262 *Hochgeschwindikeit I* (HG I)

Me 262 *Hochgeschwindikeit II* (HG II)

(Proposed V-Tail Configuration for HG II)

12 Feb. 1945 Oberammergau
Night-Fighter Proposal

Me 262 *Hochgeschwindikeit III* (HG III)

Three different Hochgeschwindikeit *(high-speed) configurations were developed by the Oberammergau Project Bureau. The HG I resembled a Me 262 with additional wing fillets and a streamlined canopy and horizontal stabilizer. The HG II used a new wing but retained much of the original fuselage. The HG III was in essence a completely new design with only the vertical stabilizer retaining any familiarity with the original Me 262. An advanced two-seat night fighter variant of the HG III was also proposed. (Dennis R. Jenkins)*

badly damaged in a ground accident and was not repaired or flown prior to the end of the war.

First proposed on 22 December 1944, the **Me 262 HG III** *Hochgeschwindikeit III* was an ambitious plan to almost totally redesign the Me 262. Two He S011 engines were buried into the root of a new highly-swept (45 degrees) wing. This proposal never progressed further than design studies, but the basic December 1944 design formed the basis for the 12 February 1945 Oberammergau night-fighter proposal. The only suggestion of its close family relationship to the Me 262 was in the use of a modified two-seat Me 262B-2 fuselage. Other changes included:

• 45 degree swept wings (46.5

(Opposite page) The first Me 262 to arrive in the United States was Werk-Nr. 111711, *which was surrendered to US forces on 31 May 1945 at Frankfurt/Rhein-Main. The aircraft had been on its first test flight from Hessental where it had been manufactured by Autobedarf Schwäbisch Hall. After a total of 10 hours and 40 minutes of flight time were accumulated in 12 test flights, the aircraft suffered an engine fire and crashed at Xenia, OH. Its pilot successfully bailed out prior to the crash. The aircraft is one of the most photographed Me 262s in the US, and is normally referred to simply as '711' or T2-711. (Air Force Museum Collection)*

Two of the six Me 262's aboard HMS Reaper on their way from Cherbourg France to Newark, New Jersey in July 1945. Also aboard were two Ar 234s, two Do 335s, three He 219s, nine Fw 190s, two Ta 152s, three Me 109s, one Me 108, one Ju 388, one Ju 88, one Doblhoff jet helicopter, and two Flettner Fl 262 helicopters. (Jay Miller Collection via the Aerospace Education Center)

degrees on the 25% MAC line),

• two Jumo 004D or two He S011 engines, submerged in the wing root,

• main undercarriage attachment at the wing roots, with the nose wheel retracting into a position in the fuselage center section beneath the cockpit,

• swept tail surfaces of the HG I initially, to be replaced later by the V-tail proposed for HG II,

• a streamlined two-seat canopy.

Although eight German aircraft were allocated US Navy BuAer Numbers in anticipation of flight tests, the only one that actually flew was an Me 262A-1a (BuNo. 121442). This aircraft had carried the Whizzers' name Screamin' Meemie, *and is now in the Air Force Museum in Dayton. (Jay Miller Collection via the Aerospace Education Center)*

The aircraft was expected to attain speeds of 650 MPH at sea level and 684 MPH at 20,000 feet. Messerschmitt kept feeling his way towards the sound barrier one step at a time. The Oberammergau Project Bureau performed extensive analysis on this design, and also carried out initial wind tunnel investigations. However, like many other futuristic studies, this design had no chance to fly prior to the end of the war.

OTHER VARIANTS

Many other versions of the Me 262 were being discussed towards the end of the war. The **Me 262D** was to have been fitted with the *Jagdfaust* anti-bomber weapon comprised of twelve rifled mortar barrels inclined forward and upward in the nose of the aircraft. Each barrel contained a 50MM RX 73 rocket fired in a single salvo when the aircraft was lined up with the belly of a bomber. Counterweights were to have been fired simultaneously from the bottom of each barrel to counter the recoil. The **Me 262E**, was to have 24 R4M rockets in the nose, plus a further 24 under each wing, fired as three salvos. Various bomber variants were also being investigated, including ones featuring internal weapons bays in bulged fuselages capable of carrying 2,205 pounds of bombs at 622 MPH.

An ultra-high-speed version of the Me 262 was proposed by Dr. Eugen Sänger in late-1944. Along with his assistant and wife, Irene Bredt, Dr. Sänger had a long history of high-speed projects, including a design for a sub-orbital *Amerika Bomber*. Sänger took a standard Me 262A-1a and added two large ramjet engines measuring 3.7 feet in

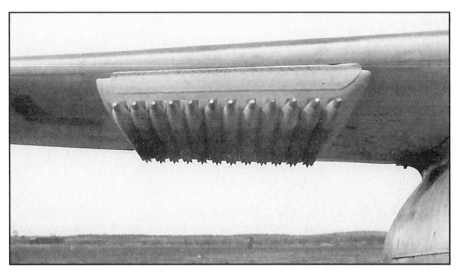

The 55MM R4M unguided air-to-air rocket proved to be a very effective anti-bomber weapon. Twelve of the rockets could be carried on a wooden rack mounted beneath each wing of some Me 262A-1a and all Me 262A-1b aircraft. Plans were in work to increase this to 24 rockets per wing, but fortunately for the Allied bombers, the war ended before this could be accomplished. (Jay Miller Collection via the Aerospace Education Center)

The most prominent feature in this photograph from the December 1945 USAAF foreign equipment report is the 'bomb release' handle on the right-side cockpit wall. This handle has been clearly marked by USAAF personnel. The circuit breaker panel is forward and radio controls are aft. (Air Force Museum Collection)

diameter and 19.2 feet long on top of each of the normal Jumo 004 nacelles. Estimated performance for the **Me 262 Lorin** included a speed of 630 MPH at sea level and a rate of climb permitting reaching 35,000 feet in less than six minutes. A major potential problem, at least from the few drawings to survive the war, was exhaust impingement on the horizontal stabilizer which was only a couple of feet directly behind the ram-jet.

The **Me 262 Mistel** was an evolution of the original Mistel which used a Bf 109 fighter attached to an unmanned, bomb-laden, Ju 88 twin-engine bomber. A version utilizing two Me 262s was submitted to the RLM on 28 November 1944, and although the RLM liked the concept, no prototype was built prior to the end of the war. A modified Me 262A-1a, constructed

This particular aircraft has additional engine instrumentation beyond what was installed in most aircraft. An additional exhaust pressure gauge flanks the normal stack of four instruments for each engine. The largest instrument at the top is the turbine tachometer, followed by the exhaust temperature, exhaust pressure, and oil pressure gauges. (Air Force Museum Collection)

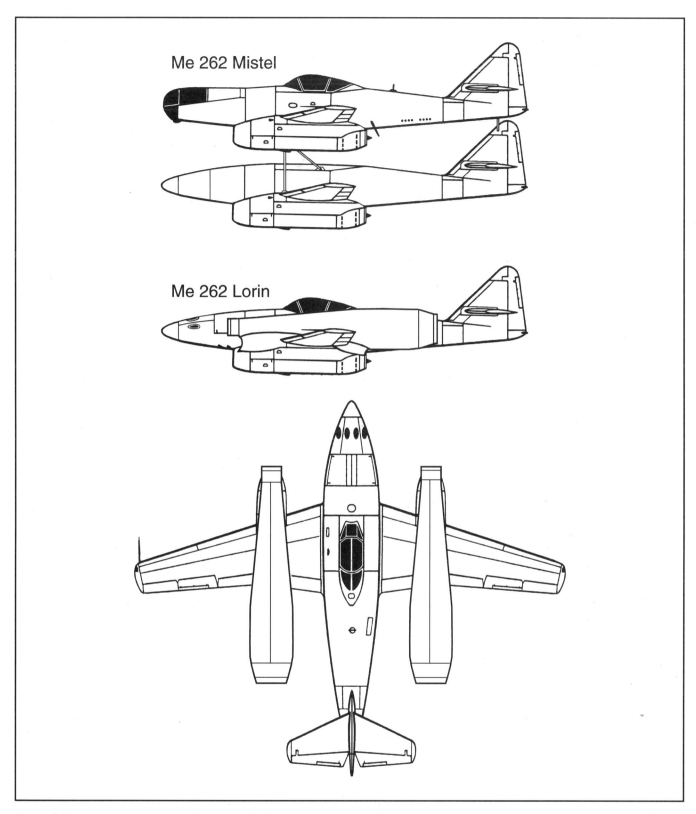

Me 262 Mistel

Me 262 Lorin

Two of the more interesting advanced Me 262 concepts. The Mistel was in essence a very expensive bomb, utilizing an entire unmanned Me 262 to deliver explosives to a target. The Lorin, envisioned by Eugen Sänger, would have used two very large ram jet engines mounted on top of the normal Jumo 004 nacelles to reach extremely high speeds. It is interesting to note that the Lorin does not seem to have included the swept back horizontal stabilizer developed for the HG series of aircraft. Exhaust impingement on the horizontals would probably have been unacceptable. (Dennis R. Jenkins)

without a cockpit or landing gear and fitted with a large shaped explosive in the nose, was to 'piggy-back' an Me 262A-2a/U2 from which the pair was controlled. A tricycle dolly was used for take-off.

Another parasite project was the Messerschmitt P.1103, a small rocket-powered interceptor armed with a single 30MM MK 108 cannon that was to be towed behind an Me 262 using the *Deichselschlepp* concept pioneered by the Me 262V10. After reaching the designated altitude, the P.1103 was to ignite its rocket motor to gain additional altitude and speed, attacking the Allied bombers from above. The P.1103 design was not completed prior to the end of the war, and no hardware had been built.

According to a report produced by Messerschmitt for the Americans in June 1945, a total of 1,443 Me 262 aircraft were produced from the delivery of the first prototype until 19 April 1945, a period of just some 14 months. Of these, 611 aircraft were damaged or lost completely through Allied bombing attacks on individual production sites and strafing attacks although 114 were repaired and returned to flight status. These numbers do not count the few machines produced by the Americans from captured parts, nor those produced in Czechoslovakia.

AVIA S-92.1

Dispersed production of the Me 262 spread into Bohemia (Czechoslovakia) towards the end of the war with the large Avia aircraft factory producing nose sections and forward fuselages, and other Czech factories producing major parts of the Jumo 004B engine. By the end of the war, Czechoslovakia held a considerable number of unused airframes, engines, and other parts for the Me 262. Looking at this considerable resource, the Czech government decided to complete a number of these aircraft to equip the Czechoslovakian Air Force.

The Letecke factory in Malesice began work on assembling the Jumo 004B-1 engines, designated M-04 by the Czechs, while the Avia plant resumed its work on the Me 262 by concentrating on 18 suitable wartime airframes. The aircraft was designated S-92 *Turbina* (the 'S' signifying 'fighter'), and was virtually identical to the Me 262A-1a. Subsequently, three additional aircraft were completed as two-seat CS-92s, nearly identical to the Me 262B-1a.

Avia Chief Test Pilot took the S-92.1 on its first flight

A nice overall shot of a fully outfitted Me 262A-2a cockpit. This aircraft had a full complement of engine instruments and bomb arming switches. The cockpit was small, causing problems for larger pilots, but this photograph is slightly exaggerated due to the lens used. (Air Force Museum Collection)

The only surviving two-seat Avia CS-92 (coded V-35) from the Czechoslovakian Air Force sits outside the VM Aviation and Space Flight Museum in Kbeli. A single-seat S-92 is also in the museum. (Jay Miller Collection via the Aerospace Education Center)

on 27 August 1946, but the aircraft was destroyed ten days later in a landing accident. The second S-92 was first flown on 24 September 1946, and one additional aircraft was completed that year. Only a single S-92 was completed in 1947, but it was nevertheless accepted by the Czech Air Force and turned over to the 5th Fighter Flight. The first two-seater, CS-92.7 flew in 1948, and all 21 aircraft had been delivered by 1950.

Various improvements were proposed by Avia, including using updated BMW 003A turbojets, and strengthening the somewhat fragile nose landing gear. Yugoslavia even considered buying S-92s in 1951. But at the public military review in Letna on 9 May 1951, six S-92s were accompanied by nine Russian Yak-23s, marking the begin-

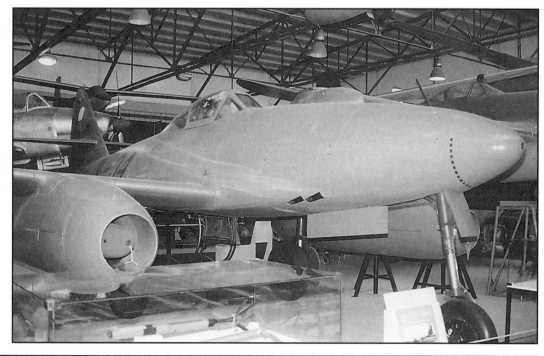

The last known remaining single-seat Avia S-92 in the VM Aviation and Space Flight Museum in Kbeli, Czechoslovakia. This aircraft was assembled from an uncompleted Me 262A-1a and used Czech-assembled Jumo 004B-2 engines, one of which sits beside it as a display. The fighter is remarkably well-preserved, as this mid-1996 photograph shows. (Henrik Clausen)

ning of closer ties to the Soviet Union. Soon afterwards, a license was issued allowing the Czechs to build the MiG-15, and the last production Me 262s would quickly fade into history. The 5th Fighter Flight was disbanded and its aircraft given to various aviation engineering schools around the Republic as teaching aids. Only two examples are known to have survived, S-92 (code V-34) and CS-92 (V-35), both in the VM Aviation and Space Flight Exhibition in Kbeli.

WATSON'S WHIZZERS

Colonel Harold E. Watson had an enviable task for anybody that enjoyed sifting through technology. He was in charge of *Project Lusty*. On 27 April 1945, General Carl Spaatz issued orders for the Air Technical Intelligence Section of the Technical Service Command of the United States Army Air Force to be formed. The unit's specific charter was to retrieve surviving *Luftwaffe* aircraft and other innovative equipment from occupied areas.

Whatever was found would be evaluated in-place, with the most interesting examples shipped back to Wright Field in Ohio for further testing. With Colonel Watson in charge, the group quickly became known as Watson's Whizzers, and the Me 262 was high on the list of desired prizes.

The area to be covered included Germany, Austria, Norway, Denmark, and France. Coordination with similar British groups prevented unnecessary duplication of effort, and another American team, this one concerned with the investigation of the A-4 (V2) rocket was also coordinated with. The Whizzers initially concentrated their efforts at Lager-Lechfeld since this was the greatest known concentration of Me 262s. In addition to the identification and retrieval of Me 262s and other aircraft, Watson managed to bring home a variety of equipment including an Enigma cryptographic machine.

Hugh Morgan covers the Whizzers in considerable detail in *Me 262: Stormbird Rising*, and the story will not be duplicated here. Suffice it to say that the recovery was interesting and well worth a reading. In all, when the HMS Reaper arrived at Newark, New Jersey, it was carrying ten Me 262s, two Ar 234s, two Do 335s, three He 219s, nine Fw 190s, two Ta 152s, three Bf 109s, one Me 108, one Ju 388, one Ju 88, one Doblhoff jet helicopter, and two Flettner Fl 262 helicopters. Colonel Watson himself, along with Captain Fred McIntosh, flew a four-engine Ju 290A transport across the Atlantic. These would keep the technical intelligence group at Wright Field busy for several years. Details of each aircraft recovered, and their use in

The main landing gear of an Me 262A-1a shows the large tread blocks used by the rough-field tires. The narrow, cylindrical device is an antenna fitted to some aircraft for the all-weather landing system. (Dennis R. Jenkins)

Allied hands, are contained in *War Prizes* by Phil Butler.

TISCHLER'S STORMBIRDS

You can not really prepare for it. If doors to the hanger used by the Texas Airplane Factory at Meacham Field in Fort Worth are open, the first thing you see are six Me 262 tails lined up in a nice neat row. It has been almost 50 years since so many Me 262s sat together in one location, and it startles you even if you know they should be there. Coming upon it without warning would be heart-stopping.

Texas Airplane Factory, owned and operated by Herbert Tischler is building brand new Me 262s. In every respect, these aircraft are better than the originals, although they remain absolutely faithful to the originals. One of the six tails you first see belongs to *Werk-Nr.* 110639, an original Me 262B-1a on loan to the Texas Airplane Factory from NAS Willow Grove. In exchange for its loan, Willow Grove will receive 110639 back in totally restored form, something it has desperately needed for many years.

Herbert Tischler was 14 years old when the Me 262V1 made its first flight. He was also fortunate and skilled enough to qualify for an RLM sponsorship at Berlin-Schöne-feld. There he learned to become a *Metallfugzeugbauer*, or metal aircraft constructor, which combined practical bench work with schooling in associated engineering subjects. This training taught Tischler how to build almost any component required on a modern aircraft, except for the engines.

The life and times of Herbert Tischler have been interesting, and a more complete history of them is contained in *Stormbird Rising* by Hugh Morgan. It is highly recommended reading. Released in 1950 from the USSR as a captured POW, Herbert joined the USAFE. In 1953, he traveled to Ecuador to work for a small regional airline before coming to the United States in 1957 to repair crashed helicopters. Tischler became self-employed in 1959, and over the next ten years his focus shifted to building airplanes.

In the next 12 years Tischler would make a name for himself constructing various reproduction vintage aircraft, including a 70-per-cent-scale P-51, a full-size Curtiss P-6E biplane fighter (currently on display at the EAA Museum in Oshkosh), and a Boeing P-12 fighter which is currently displayed at the Museum of Flight in Seattle. The Texas Airplane Factory was created to fill an order for four Grumman F3F-2s ordered by museum owners,

The nose of Me 262B-1a Werk-Nr. 110639 after being restored by Tischler. The nose section was made of steel, and had suffered greatly from being outdoors for four decades. The compact 30MM MK 108 cannon reproduction is visible at lower right, and also inside the plexiglass covering the cannon access door on 110639. (Dennis R. Jenkins)

The fuselage of Werk-Nr. 110639 at Tischler's following restoration. Stacked up in front of it are horizontal stabilizers and rudders for the reproduction aircraft. A single piece of the new casting for the replica Jumo 004s is in the foreground. (Dennis R. Jenkins)

The Me 262B-1a (Werk-Nr. 110639) as it looked in April 1970 outside at NAS Willow Grove. The paint scheme is decidedly non-standard, although at this point the aircraft does not look terribly the worse for sitting outside. This was not the case when it arrived at Tischler's rusting and in dire need of restoration. (Jay Miller Collection via the Aerospace Education Center)

including Doug Champlin from Mesa, Arizona.

In July 1993 Herb Tischler and his troupe of sheet metal workers, machinists, and mechanics began the process of manufacturing five flyable Me 262s. Four of these aircraft will be two-seaters based on the Me 262B-1a and one will be a single-seater Me 262A-1a. Two of the two-seaters will contain a system that enable them to be rapidly converted between the two configurations (although they will always carry the lower fuel capacity of the two-seater).

The new Me 262s are virtually indistinguishable from the original, other than they are obviously 50 years newer. The materials and construction techniques are as authentic as possible, although the quality greatly surpasses the mostly unskilled labor employed by Messerschmitt during the war. The only major difference will be the engines. Since Jumo 004Bs are no longer available, and it was not a particularly reliable powerplant anyway, Tischler has elected to use General Electric J-85-GE-17A engines from the A-37. To maintain the proper appearance, the Texas Airplane Factory will house the new engines in replicas of the original Jumo 004B. This serves two purposes. First, the J-85 weighs 1,500 pounds less than the Jumo, and the cast replica will help restore the correct balance and center-of-gravity to the aircraft. Second, anyone opening the engine nacelles will be greeted by what should be there … a Jumo 004B. Of course, another result of the new engines, the new owners will have almost 50% more thrust to play with!

When I visited the Texas Airplane Factory with Jay Miller in April 1996, all of the epoxy primered fuselages were sitting in jigs, one set of wings was being constructed, the cockpit liners for all the aircraft were nearing completion, various engine casting were being worked, and a couple of pallets of tires had just arrived. The shop was extremely neat, clean, and well organized. Detailed comparisons between the new aircraft and *Werk-Nr.* 110639 failed to reveal any significant differences, and the amount of restoration to this aircraft is also apparent. The Tischler's are on track for a first flight in late 1997—the first time an Me 262 will have flown in over 50 years. It should prove to be an interesting event.

NAKAJIMA KIKKA

The Japanese Navy's Nakajima

A canopy is fitted to the #4 Tischler airplane. The tail section has not been fitted yet, showing the triangular fuselage cross-section. (Dennis R. Jenkins)

Kikka (Orange Blossom) was a twin-jet fighter loosely based on the Messerschmitt Me 262. The *Kikka* was the only Japanese jet-powered aircraft produced during World War II that was capable of taking off on its own power, although it did so only twice. A second type of jet-powered aircraft, the Army's Nakajima Ki.201 *Karyu*, was in the early phases of development.

At the beginning of 1944, the Germans first revealed details of the Me 262 to the Japanese in Berlin. The reports on the progress of the Me 262 received from the Japanese air attache in Berlin led the Naval Staff to instruct the Nakajima Hikoki K.K. to design a single-seat twin-jet attack fighter based on the Me 262. Requirements included a maximum speed of 431 MPH, a range of 127 miles with a 1,102-pound bomb load or 173 miles with a 551-pound bomb load. Take-off was to take no more than 1,150 feet using two 992 LBF assist

rockets. Provisions were to be made for the aircraft to have folding wings so it could be hidden in caves and tunnels, and an EMPHasis was to be placed on a simple design that could be produced with unskilled labor.

By July 1944 the Germans had agreed to allow the Japanese to manufacture both the Me 163 and the Me 262. Blueprints and drawings for both aircraft, their engines, and fuels were sent to Japan aboard different U-boats. On 22 July 1944, Göring approved delivering one Me 163 and one Me 262 to the Japanese as sample aircraft, although this was later dropped since there was no practical way to transport the aircraft to Japan. However, although the Me 163 plans reached Japan, the Me 262 plans were delayed, then finally, the U-boat they were on was captured by Allied forces on 16 May 1945, eight days after Germany surrendered.

So the Japanese were faced with reconstructing the design from the memory of various engineers that had been to Germany, and from various preliminary German documents that had reached Japan. The overall configuration of the *Kikka* was quite similar to that of the Me 262, but the *Kikka* was slightly smaller than its German counterpart. Also, the aircraft used essentially unswept wings, and a somewhat boxier fuselage cross-section. Like the Me 262, the twin turbojets were mounted in separate nacelles underneath the wings. Initially, the aircraft was to be powered by a pair of 441 LBF thrust Tsu-11 Campini-type engines, but these were soon replaced by two 750 LBF Japanese-designed Ne-12 turbojets. However, the Ne-12 failed to deliver the expected thrust, and official interest in the *Kikka* began to wane because it appeared that it would be unable to meet its performance requirements. In the meantime, photographs of the German BMW

The nose is test fitted to the #3 Tischler airplane. Each fuselage has its own support jigs, allowing production to take place simultaneously. (Dennis R. Jenkins)

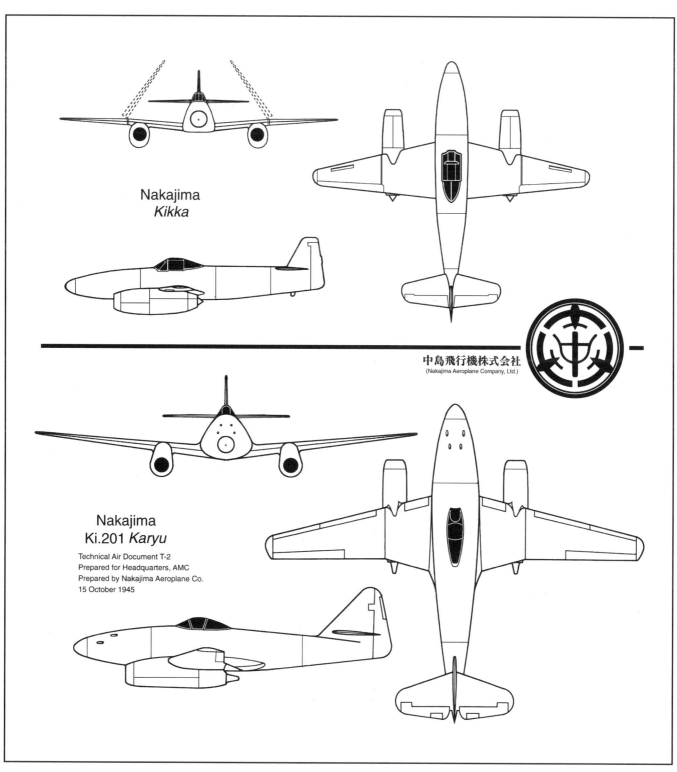

Nakajima
Kikka

中島飛行機株式会社
(Nakajima Aeroplane Company, Ltd.)

Nakajima
Ki.201 *Karyu*

Technical Air Document T-2
Prepared for Headquarters, AMC
Prepared by Nakajima Aeroplane Co.
15 October 1945

The Nakajima Kikka *and* Karyu *were originally intended to be copies of the Me 262. However, all of the technical data the German's sent did not reach Japan in time to support the development of the aircraft. The* Kikka *was designed mostly from the memory of several Japanese engineers that had received preliminary briefings on the Me 262. It was a good deal smaller and did not seriously resemble the German aircraft except in overall configuration. Noteworthy are the folding wings intended to allow storage in caves and tunnels. A single* Kikka *flew prior to the end of the war, and several other prototypes were nearing completion. The* Karyu *was much closer in appearance to the Me 262, but no actual manufacturing was completed on the first prototype prior to the end of the war.*
(Dennis R. Jenkins)

The sole remaining Kikka *as it hangs in the National Air and Space Museum's facility in Silver Hill, Maryland. The engine nacelles are not original, and the control surfaces need recovered. (Jay Miller Collection via the Aerospace Education Center)*

The Kikka *Final assembly line on 6 November 1945 at Nakajima's Koizui plant. In the background are unfinished 4-engine Renzan Navy bombers. Near the end of the war, all effort stopped on the Renzan's so that labor and material could be concentrated on the production of the Kikka. (Air Force Museum Collection)*

003 turbojet had been obtained, and the Japanese were able to use these photos to assist them in designing a similar turbojet (designated Ne-20) rated at 1,047 LBF thrust. It was decided to switch the *Kikka* to the Ne-20, and since it now appeared that the performance requirements could be met after all, the project moved forward rapidly.

The first *Kikka* made its first flight on 7 August at Kisarazu Naval Air Base with Susumu Takaoka at the controls. The second flight, which took place four days later, had to be aborted during takeoff because the two assist rockets were mounted at an incorrect angle. The Japanese surrender brought an immediate termination to the project on 15 August 1945. At the time of termination, a second prototype was almost ready for flight trials and 18 additional prototypes and pre-production aircraft were in various stages of assembly. At least one, and possibly as many as three, air-craft were brought to the United States after the war, although none were reassembled for flight. One of these is in storage at the National Air and Space Museum.

The estimated performance included a maximum speed of 387 MPH at sea level and 433 MPH at 32,810 feet. The service ceiling was 39,370 feet, with a climb to 32,180 feet taking 26 minutes. Range was estimated at 586 miles with a combat load. The *Kikka* had a wing span of 32.8 feet, was 26.6 feet long, and 9.7 feet high. The wing provided 141.1 square feet of area. The aircraft weighed 5,071 pounds empty, 7,716 pounds loaded, and had a maximum take-off weight of 8,995 pounds. None of the prototypes carried any armament. Fighter, trainer, reconnaissance, and attack versions of the *Kikka* were planned. The bomber version was to be unarmed, but the fighter version was to carry a pair of 30MM cannon. Production versions would have had two 1,984 LBF thrust Ne-130 axial-flow turbojets.

The Army's Nakajima Ki.201 *Karyu* was in response to a 12 January 1945 requirement for an attack fighter with performance equal or better than that of contemporary jet fighters. The first aircraft, designed by a team led by Iwao Shibuya, was to be completed by December 1945, with 18 production aircraft delivered by March 1946.

The aircraft was to be powered by two Ne 230 engines, and carry two 20MM and two 30MM cannon. A single 1,102-pound bomb was to be carried. Additional equipment included the TaKi-15 airborne intercept radar, indicating the aircraft was to be capable of more than simple attack missions. The prototype was to be assembled at Nakajima's Mitaka plant on the west edge of Tokyo, but when Japan collapsed the final design was less than 50% completed, and no hardware had been built.

Two *Kikkas on the assembly line at the end of the war. The large cavity in the bottom of the fuselage is where the fuel tank was installed. The wing was hinged just outboard of the engine nacelle so that it could fold for storage in caves and tunnels.* (Air Force Museum Collection)

GLOSSARY

AUFKLÄRUNG
Reconnaissance

BMW
Bavarian Motor Werks

BRAMO
Brandenburg Engine Werks (division of BMW)

DEICHSELSCHLEPP
Pole-tow. Can refer to bombs or fuel

DIPL. ING.
Diploma in Engineering

EINSATZKOMMANDO
Operational Detachment

ERGÄNZUNGS-JAGDGESCHWADER (EJG)
Fighter Replacement Group

ERPROBUNGSKOMMANDO (EKDO)
Test Detachment

ERPROBUNGSSTELLE RECHLIN
Test Pilot School

FELDWEBEL
Equal to Sergeant in RAF or Airman First Class in USAAF

FLETTNER
Auxiliary moveable portion of a control surface

FLUGZEUGFÜHRERSCHULE
Pilot Training School

FLIEGER
Airman or Pilot

FLUGKAPITÄN
Honorary title bestowed by the *Luftwaffe* on highly-regarded civilian test pilots

FUNKGERÄT (FUG)
Radio or Radar set

GENERAL
Equal to Air Marshal in RAF or Lieutenant General in USAAF

GENERAL DER JAGDFLIEGER
General of the Fighter Forces

GENERALLEUTNANT
Equal to Air Vice-Marshal in RAF or Major General in USAAF

GENERALMAJOR
Equal to Air Commodore in RAF or Brigadier General in USAAF

GESCHWADER
Fighter Wing, usually consisting of three *Gruppen*, with a single *Stab* unit

GMBH
Limited liability company

GRUPPE
Equal to a Wing in the RAF

HAUPTMANN
Equal to a Flight Lieutenant in RAF or Captain in USAAF

HWK
Hellmuth Walter Werks

IFF
Identification, Friend or Foe

JABO
Fighter-Bomber (diminutive from *Jagd bomber*)

JAGDFLIEGER
Fighter Pilot

JAGDFLIEGERSCHULE
Fighter Training School

JAGDESCHWADER (JG)
Fighter Wing

JUMO
Junkers Motorenbau

KAMPFGESCHWADER (KG)
Battle or Bomber Wing

KOMMANDO (KDO)
Detachment, often named after its commanding officer

KOMMANDUER
Commanding Officer

MAJOR
Equal to Squadron Leader in RAF, or Major in USAAF

MG
Machine Gun

MK
Machine Cannon

NAHAUFKLÄRUNGSGRUPPE (NAGR)
Short-Range Reconnaissance unit

NACHTJAGDGESCHWADER (NJG)
Night-Fighter Group

OBERBEFEHLSHABER DER LUFTWAFFE (OB.D.L)
Commander in Chief of the *Luftwaffe*

OBERFELDWEBEL
Equal to Flight Sergeant in RAF or Master Sergeant in USAAF

OBERLEUTNANT
Equal to Flying Officer in RAF or Lieutenant in USAAF

OBERST
Equal to Group Captain in RAF or Colonel in USAAF

OBERSTLEUTNANT
Equal to Wing Commander in RAF or Lieutenant Colonel in USAAF

OBERKOMMANDO DER LUFTWAFFE
Luftwaffe High Command

REVI
Reflector gun-sight

REICHSLUFTFÄHRTMINISTERIUM (RLM)
German Ministry of Aviation

REICHSMARSCHALL
Unique title for Hermann Göring

SCHRÄGE MUSIK
Fixed weapons firing upwards and obliquely

SCHWALBE
Swallow. Nickname for Me 262 fighter variants

SONDERTREIBWERKE
Pre-production aircraft (S-series)

STAB
Staff or Staff Group

STAFFEL
Equal to a Squadron in RAF

STAFFELKAPITÄN
Commander of a squadron

STURMVOGEL
Stormbird. Nickname for Me 262 fighter-bombers

TECHNISCHES AMT
Technical Department of the RLM

TL-STRAHLTRIEBWERKE
Turbojet engine

UNTEROFFIZIER
Equal to Corporal in RAF or Corporal in USAAF

VERSUCHS OR VERSUCHSMUSTER
Experimental aircraft (V-series)

WILDE SAU
Wild Boar. Method of night-fighting devised by Halo Hermann

ZERSTÖRERGESCHWADER
Destroyer

ZWIEBEL
Onion (exhaust cone on aft-end of engine nacelle)

SIGNIFICANT DATES

1909
Several French patents issued for turbojet engine concepts.

1930
Frank Whittle receives British patent #347206 for an axial-flow turbojet engine design.

10 NOVEMBER 1935
Hans Joachim Pabst von Ohain receives German patent #317/38 for a jet engine he developed as a student at Göttingen University.

OCTOBER 1937
Messerschmitt conducts in-house trade studies on possible jet-powered aircraft.

AUTUMN 1938
The *Technisches Amt* of the *Reichsluftfährtministerium* approaches Willy Messerschmitt and Ernst Heinkel to study possible aircraft based on jet power.

7 JUNE 1939
Messerschmitt and Heinkel submit their proposals to the RLM. The Messerschmitt proposal is known as *Projekt 1065*.

27 AUGUST 1939
The experimental Heinkel He 178 makes the first flight of a jet-powered aircraft in Germany.

9 NOVEMBER
1939 Messerschmitt submits a revised proposal for their jet fighter.

19 DECEMBER 1939
A preliminary mock-up of the P.1065 is reviewed by the RLM.

1 MARCH 1940
After a further examination of mock-ups by the RLM, Messerschmitt receives a contract for three flyable Me 262 prototypes and a static test article.

15 MAY 1940
The Me 262 design is revised with swept wings and under-slung engine nacelles.

JULY 1940
Advanced development of the Jumo 004 engines begins.

AUGUST 1940
Manufacturing of Me 262 subsystems begins.

JANUARY 1941
Final assembly of the first Me 262 prototype.

2 APRIL 1941
The Heinkel He 280 makes its first flight.

17 APRIL 1941
The Me 262 makes its first flight powered by a Jumo 210Ga piston engine. The maximum speed attained by *Flugkapitän* Fritz Wendel is 261 MPH.

17 APRIL 1941
The Heinkel H2 280 sets a world's speed record of 485 MPH.

11 MAY 1941
The British Gloster E28/39 Meteor jet fighter makes its first flight.

DECEMBER 1941
The Jumo 004 jet engine completes a ten hour ground test at 1,453 LBF thrust.

25 MARCH 1942
The first Me 262 takes prototype takes-off under jet power for the first time using BMW 003 engines. And almost crashes due to dual engine failure.

18 JULY 1942
The third prototype Me 262 becomes the first to fly with the new Jumo 004 engines. Fritz Wendel is again at the controls and attains 375 MPH. A second flight is made later the same day.

11 AUGUST 1942
The first Me 262 flight by a *Luftwaffe* pilot almost ends in tragedy when Henrich Beauvais hits an unfortunately placed pile of manure at the end of the runway. Beauvais was not seriously injured although the aircraft was heavily damaged.

2 OCTOBER 1942
The American Bell XP-59A Airacomet jet fighter makes its first flight.

JANUARY 1943
The Allies receive reconnaissance data on a prototype Me 262 at Augsburg.

11 FEBRUARY 1943
An Me 262 fuselage is dropped from the Me 323S9 into the Chiemsee in an effort to obtain information on its flutter characteristics. A second drop is conducted on 23 October 1943.

20 MARCH 1943
Hauptmann Wolfgang Späte becomes the first operational *Luftwaffe* pilot to fly the Me 262, and is highly impressed by the speed of the aircraft.

18 APRIL 1943
Wilhelm Ostertag is killed in the first fatal accident involving an Me 262.

SIGNIFICANT DATES

2 JUNE 1943
The Me 262 is ordered into production as a fighter with a goal of 60 aircraft per month.

26 JUNE 1943
The Me 262V5 flies for the first time equipped with a tricycle landing gear.

25 JULY 1943
The Me 262V4 is successfully demonstrated to Hermann Göring.

2 NOVEMBER 1943
Hermann Göring visits the Messerschmitt works at Augsburg and inquires about the Me 262's ability to carry bombs. He is assured it can.

DECEMBER 1943
Albert Speer gives the Me 262 the highest production priority in the *Reich*.

8 JANUARY 1944
The American Lockheed XP-80 Shooting Star jet fighter makes its first flight.

JANUARY 1944
23 Me 262 airframes sit complete except for engines.

SPRING 1944
American P-51 Mustangs begin to escort heavy bombers all the way to Berlin.

APRIL 1944
Deliveries to the *Luftwaffe* finally begin with 16 delivered during April and 7 more in May. *Erprobungskommandos 262* is established to perform service trials on the new aircraft.

23 MAY 1944
Hitler orders production of the Me 262 to concentrate on fighter-bomber variants. All fighter production is to cease, and existing aircraft converted into fighter-bombers.

6 JUNE 1944
Allied troops come ashore at Normandy beach. Less than 30 Me 262s were in operational service. None could carry bombs.

JULY 1944
The first Me 262B two-seat trainer is delivered from Blöhm und Voss.

JULY 1944
The first Me 262 fighter-bomber variant is delivered to the *Luftwaffe*.

6 JULY 1944
An Me 262 breaks the 1,000 KPH (624 MPH) 'barrier,' becoming the first aircraft to intentionally fly so fast.

26 JULY 1944
Leutnant Alfred Schreiber from *Kommando Thierfelder* scores the first aerial victory by a jet fighter by downing an RAF Mosquito.

AUGUST 1944
Kommando Schenk performs operational fighter-bomber sorties over France.

10 AUGUST 1944
10 prototypes and 112 production Me 262s had been produced, but fewer than 50 are in operational service.

28 AUGUST 1944
USAAF Major Joseph Myers and Lieutenant M. D. Croy, Jr. are credited with the first confirmed kill of an Me 262.

30 AUGUST 1944
Hitler agrees that every 20th Me 262 can be produced as a fighter.

10 JANUARY 1945
Over 600 Me 262s had been produced, but only 61 were in operational service.

27 JANUARY 1945
The Me 262C-1a rocket-assisted test aircraft climbs 26,250 feet in 4.5 minutes, achieving a top speed of 629 MPH.

3 MARCH 1945
The first concentrated Me 262 attack sends 29 jet fighters against American bomber formations.

18 MARCH 1945
A total of 37 Me 262s attack formations containing 1,221 bombers escorted by 632 fighters. Twelve bombers and two fighters are destroyed with the loss of two Me 262s.

APRIL 1945
More than 1,200 Me 262s had been accepted by the *Luftwaffe*, but fewer than 200 are in operational service.

10 APRIL 1945
The 55 sorties flown by Me 262s will mark the greatest number of missions flown in a single day. Ten heavy bombers fall, but the Americans shoot down 27 jet fighters.

27 AUGUST 1946
The first Czechoslovakian Avia S.92 makes its first flight.

JULY 1993
The Texas Airplane Factory begins assembly of five new flyable Me 262s.

LATE 1997
The first of the new Me 262s should make its first flight.